ANTRYM &DOWNE
The Scale of English miles.
The Scale of Irish miles.
Performed by John Speede London An 1610
COUNTYE ANTRYM
THE ROWTE
Sok le Boy
Lough Neaugh
The Nether Clan de Boy
Knockfergus
Knockfergus Bay
DOWNE
Lecale
Mourne
Newry
Bagnall
Kilultagh
Kilwarlin
ARDES
IRISH SEA
SCOTLAND
The Raghlins
Carrogh
Mc Guilly
Clan Brassil

SEARCHING FOR
SCOTCH-IRISH ROOTS
IN
SCOTTISH RECORDS
1600–1750

By
David Dobson

CLEARFIELD

Printed for
Clearfield Company by
Genealogical Publishing Co.
Baltimore, Maryland
2007

ISBN-13: 978-0-8063-5317-3
ISBN-10: 0-8063-5317-1

Made in the United States of America

CONTENTS

PREFACE

The aim of this book is to identify source material in Scottish libraries and archives that could enable people of Scotch-Irish ancestry, otherwise known as the Ulster-Scots, to locate their Scottish roots.

The need for such a publication has become increasingly obvious. As interest in genealogy and family history has expanded, there has been an increase in resources to satisfy that demand, such as books, journals, and CD ROMs, plus societies and access to archival material. Such source material, both primary and secondary, is scattered throughout scores of libraries and archives; thus much of it remains unfamiliar to the average researcher. Family historians in Ireland, as well as those researchers of Scotch-Irish ancestry living overseas, may well wish to make the link over the sea to Scotland. Unfortunately, they may often be unaware of what resources are available and where these records may be found.

This book aims to provide the answers to such questions. There are certainly records in Scotland that are likely to supply links with Ireland from the Plantation period onwards; however, many of them are still in their original manuscript form, which may pose paleographic problems for the average researcher. The handwriting problem may be alleviated through the study of books or websites designed for that purpose, while the archaic words will be found in Scots dictionaries that are generally to hand in libraries and archives in Scotland. Linking one's Scotch-Irish ancestor to one's origins in Scotland is certainly challenging, but it is not an impossible task.

David Dobson
St. Andrews, Scotland
2006

INTRODUCTION

Since the twelfth century, the kings of England laid claim to Ireland and attempted to settle English colonists there. This strategy was opposed by the indigenous population, who for centuries struggled with the invaders. The only notable Scottish presence in Ireland during the medieval period was from 1315 to 1318 when King Robert the Bruce, who had successfully driven the English out of Scotland, sent an army to assist the Irish in their fight against the English. However, the English held firm and gradually intensified their hold, especially in the south-east of Ireland. The Protestant Reformation of the mid-sixteenth century added to the problem, with the native Irish and many of the English settlers (the so-called "Old English") remaining loyal to Roman Catholicism.

Scottish settlement in Ireland dates from the late sixteenth century. In that period, warriors from the West Highlands of Scotland, the "galloglasses," came to Ulster to aid the Irish in their struggle against Queen Elizabeth I's forces. These "galloglasses" (from the Gaelic "gall-oglach," meaning foreign warriors) were Gaelic-speaking Catholic Highlanders and thus were almost indistinguishable from the native Irish. Many of them were McDonnells, and their septs came mainly from Argyllshire.

On the death of Elizabeth of England in 1603, the king of Scotland, James VI, became King James I of England as well. He inherited the Irish problem and decided to resolve it by settling substantial number of English and Scots in Ulster. In 1607 a number of native lords of Ulster, the indigenous elite of the province, abandoned their lands there and fled to continental Europe. Under the feudal system their lands then reverted to the Crown. Consequently, King James planned an organized settlement of Ulster as had occurred in Munster during the sixteenth century. The plan was to divide the available lands into estates ranging in size from 1,000 to 3,000 acres that were to be granted to land-lords who would be responsible for settling Scottish and English immigrants thereon and developing the land by building towns and farms. Many of these landlords, known as "undertakers," originated in the Scottish Lowlands and in the south-west counties in particular. They, in turn, recruited settlers largely from their own existing estates or places of residence in Scotland. The main counties in Scotland from which these Scots settlers for Ulster were recruited were Kirkcudbrightshire, Wigtownshire, Ayrshire, Renfrewshire, Dumfries-shire, and Lanarkshire. Soon Scottish settlers could be found throughout the province of Ulster, especially in the counties of Antrim, Londonderry, Tyrone, Donegal, Fermanagh, Armagh, and Cavan. Thus the Crown effectively drove an English-speaking Protestant wedge between the Catholic Irish and their co-religionists in the Highlands of Scotland.

The next milestone in the process of the Scottish migration to Ulster was the War of the Three Kingdoms (known to Anglo-centric historians as the English Civil War) that began in 1638 and ended in 1651. The Irish dimension was the 1641 Rising. The initial success of the Irish "rebels" resulted in a Scottish Covenanter Army arriving in Ulster in 1642 to defend the Protestant settlers. While a number of the early seventeenth-century Scottish settlers had been Episcopalian and a handful Catholics, from the 1640s on the vast majority were of the Presbyterian persuasion. The army chaplains that arrived with the Scots army in 1642 established the Presbyterian Church as the predominant church of the Scottish settlers in Ireland. By 1690 the Synod of Ulster was created, which represented one-hundred and twenty congregations out of a population of nearly 150,000 Scots and their descendants.

During the second half of the seventeenth century, immigrants from Scotland flowed steadily into Ulster. Some arrived as refugees, such as the Covenanters who fled from Scotland during "the killing time," while others arrived to escape the famines that ravaged much of Scotland during the 1690s, and a few were Borders reivers escaping justice. During the Restoration period, the Stuart kings of England attempted to impose Episcopacy on the Church of Scotland to which a largely hostile Presbyterian Scotland responded with armed rebellion. The government met the rebellion with draconian reaction such as execution and enforced transportation, in turn causing an exodus to America, Holland, and Ireland especially during the 1680s.

In 1688 the Catholic King James II abandoned his throne, fled to France, and was replaced by the Protestants William and Mary. In Ireland, the Earl of Antrim raised a Jacobite army in support of King James and besieged Londonderry. James arrived in Ireland with French support in 1689, but he was defeated by the forces of William and Mary at the Battle of the Boyne in 1690.

Although the Presbyterian Scots-Irish had given their full support to the Crown during the Williamite Wars, they were subsequently treated as second-class citizens in Ireland by the English establishment. Presbyterian and other Dissenting ministers were not recognized by the State, and all public office holders were required to be Episcopalian or Anglicans, while the Presbyterians were required to pay tithes to finance the Episcopal Church of Ireland. Such facts, together with changing economic circumstances and rent-racking, contributed to the great Scotch-Irish or Ulster Scot emigrations of the eighteenth century that started with a movement to New England in 1718.

Over the course of the eighteenth century, the Ulster Scots would become the single most numerous ethnic group to settle in colonial America.

While the overseas descendents of the Ulster Scots have a substantial challenge in tracking their ancestors back to Ireland, there is even a more difficult challenge awaiting those that wish there is even a more difficult challenge awaiting those that wish to research their Scottish origins. One of the best books in print for those wishing to trace their Irish ancestry is Margaret Dickson Falley's *Irish and Scotch-Irish Ancestral Research* [Genealogical Publishing, Baltimore, 1998]. For those interested in their Ulster-Scot ancestry, the latest publication in this field is William J. Roulston's *Researching Scots-Irish Ancestors. The Essential Genealogical Guide to Early Modern Ulster, 1600-1800* [Ulster Historical Foundation, Belfast, 2005]. However, while these books provide invaluable information on genealogical research in Ulster, there is nothing in print committed to records in Scotland relating to the Scottish participation in the Plantation of Ulster during the seventeenth century. This book is designed to identify the sources that do, or are likely to, contain material of relevance to those wishing to find the origins of the Ulster-Scots. The majority of the settlers from Scotland to Ulster left little evidence of their origins; however, there is a limited amount of evidence scattered throughout manuscripts and some published works held in libraries and archives throughout Scotland, especially in the south-west.

ACKNOWLEDGMENTS

The illustrations and extracts used in this publication appear with the kind permission of the Keeper of the Records of the National Archives of Scotland, the Scottish Records Society, and the University of St. Andrews Library.

CHAPTER ONE
Church Records

This chapter deals with records of the Church of Scotland beginning with the Old Parish Registers of Baptisms and Marriages. Prior to the Census records as from 1841 and the statutory registers of births, marriages and deaths dating from 1855, the Old Parish Registers are the primary sources of information on baptisms and marriages in Scotland. While a few date back to the sixteenth century, the majority are much later; a considerable number of parish registers of the Lowlands date from the seventeenth century, while those of Highland parishes are generally from the eighteenth century onwards. Within the region—comprising the neighbouring counties of Dumfries-shire, Ayrshire, Kirkcudbrightshire, Wigtownshire, Renfrewshire, and Lanarkshire, from where the majority of the Scots settlers in Ulster are believed to have originated—there are nearly two hundred parishes. Of these, Strathaven in Lanarkshire has the oldest parish registers that date from 1576. [See New Register House.OPR#621] Throughout the region as a whole, there are eighty-nine parish registers that date from the seventeenth century and ninety three dating from the eighteenth century. All these have been microfilmed and indexed. Microfiche indexes exists such as the Old Parish Register index, based solely on the church records, and the International Genealogical Index, which incorporates the church records and contains records from other sources. The Old Parish Registers are to be found in New Register House, Edinburgh, though in practice the originals are rarely made available. Microfilm copies are available there and in local libraries throughout the land. The records of baptisms and marriages held in Church of Scotland parish kirks can also be found on the website www.scotlandspeople.com. Virtually all the Scots who settled in seventeenth century Ulster would have been baptised in the Church of Scotland and may well appear in the parish records where they survive, though records for the early seventeenth century are far from comprehensive.

Possibly the second most useful of the records of the Church of Scotland, as far as genealogists are concerned, are the Kirk Session

Records. While the Old Parish Registers of baptism and marriage are familiar to, and well used by, family historians the Kirk Session Records are less so. Basically this source represents the records kept by the minister and the elders of each parish as they attempted to maintain discipline over the congregations, record mort-cloth dues (which provide evidence of death), also note how funds were raised and dispersed particularly to the poor. The Kirk Session records are to be found in the National Archives of Scotland; these are all in their original un-indexed manuscript form, though a handful have been published; for example, *Inverness Kirk Session Register, 1661-1800*, [A. Mitchell, Inverness, 1902], or *Mouswald Kirk Session Minutes: 1640-1659*, by A.E. Truckell, in *Transactions of the Dumfries-shire and Galloway Natural History and Antiquarian Society*, 3rd series, volume lxxvii, [DGNHAS; Dumfries, 2003], pp.167-180.

The Kirk Session Records of the parishes of south west Scotland are likely to contain references to people bound for or coming from Ireland and to people resident in Ulster with whom there is some local connection. Take Dumfries Kirk Session Register (NAS.CH2.537) as an example. There are Records of charitable payments to poor people who had come from Ireland to Scotland in 1690: Matthew Young was given £1.8 shillings on 16 January, while William Carruthers, also from Ireland, received one dollar. The 1690s was a period of a relatively large scale migration from Scotland to Ireland due largely to harvest failures. Churches in Scotland on the route to Ireland dispensed charity to poor travellers; for example, on 2 October 1690 Patrick Hume and his wife, bound for Ireland, were given £2 by the parishioners of Dumfries to help them on their way there. As mentioned, one of the main tasks of the Kirk Sessions was to maintain discipline in the parishes; and their efforts are recorded in the Kirk Session records. These, too, may have Irish links; for example, on 11 July 1692 James Fulton was accused by Dumfries Kirk Session of having bigamously married Agnes Currie in Dumfries, despite the fact that he had a wife and three children in Antrim. Some husbands seem to have absconded and gone abroad, men like David Sloan, a baker journeyman in Dumfries, who married

Jean Glover but deserted her and went to Ireland by 21 March 1765. The Kirk Sessions also were responsible for ensuring that errant fathers were made responsible for their wives and for their children, otherwise the cost would fall on the community at large.

While the obvious places to locate entries recording baptisms and marriages are the parochial baptismal and marriage registers, a few may be found within the kirk session registers. Diane Baptie has identified them in her *Parish Registers in the Kirk Session Record of the Church of Scotland.* [Scottish Association of Family History Societies, Aberdeen, 2001] Among those of south western Scotland dating before 1750 are: Galston, Ayrshire, dating from 1568 [NAS.CH2.1335/1/4/8/22]; Applegarth and Sibbaldie, Dumfriesshire, dating from 1694 [NAS.CH2.1220/1/2]; and Rutherglen, Lanarkshire, dating from 1663 [NAS.CH2.315/1/8/9]. While most are to be found in the NAS, a few are in local archives, particularly the Glasgow Archives and the Ayr Archives.

Kirk Session Records of south-west Scotland parishes now in the National Archives of Scotland include:

Applegarth and Sibbaldbie [NAS.CH2/1220] from 1694

Avendale [NAS.CH2/930] from 1660

Ayr [NAS.CH2.751] from 1604

Beith [NAS.CH2/31] from 1701

Biggar [NAS.CH2/1253] from 1523

Blantyre [NAS.CH2/916] from 1693

Cadder [NAS.CH2/863] from 1688

Cambuslang [NAS.CH2.415] from 1658

Carluke [NAS.CH2/56] from 1645

Carmichael [NAS.CH2/57] from 1694

Carmunnock [NAS.CH2/58] from 1694

Carnock [NAS.CH2/59] from 1699

Carstairs [NAS.CH2/63] from 1672

Covington & Thankerton [NAS.CH2/72] from 1652

Crawfordjohn [NAS.CH2.397] from 1693

Cumnock [NAS.CH2/81] from 1704

Dailly [NAS.CH2.392] from 1691

Dalry [NAS.CH2/1328] from 1693

Douglas [NAS.CH2/953] from 1692

Dumfries [NAS.CH2.537] from 1648

Dundonald [NAS.CH2/104] from 1602

Dunoon and Kilmun [NAS.CH2.456] from 1667

Eastwood [NAS.CH2.119] from 1689

Ecclesmachan [NAS.CH2.623] from 1662

Gargunnock [NAS.CH2/1121] from 1625

Girthon [NAS.CH2/1526] from 1694

Barony, Glasgow [NAS.CH2/173] from 1676

St Mungo's Cathedral, Glasgow, [NAS.CH2.550] from 1583

Glencairn [NAS.CH2.617] from 1693

Govan [NAS.CH2/1277] from 1651

Irvine [NAS.CH2/197] from 1646

Jedburgh [NAS.CH2.552] from 1672

Kilbirnie [NAS.CH2/208] from 1688

Kilmarnock, Laigh [NAS.CH2/1252] from 1646

Kilwinning [NAS.CH2.591] from 1656

Kingarth [NAS.CH2/219] from 1648

Kirkcudbright [NAS.CH2.520] from 1692

Kirkoswald [NAS.CH2.562] from 1617

Kirkpatrick-Durham [NAS.CH2/231] from 1694

Kirkpatrick Juxta [NAS.CH2.705] from 1692

Kirkpatick-Irongray [NAS.CH2/1343] from 1691

Lanark [NAS.CH2/1529] from 1699

Lesmahagow [NAS.CH2/239] from 1651

Lilliesleaf [NAS.CH2/241] from 1649

Lochrutton [NAS.CH2/1344] from 1697

Lochwinnoch [NAS.CH2.649] from 1691

Mauchline [NAS.CH2/896] from 1669

Monckton [NAS.CH2.809] from 1615

Monigaff [NAS.CH2/1404] from 1694

Nenthorn [NAS.CH2/1323] from 1696

New Luce [NAS.CH2.700] from 1694

Ochiltree [NAS.CH2.778] from 1695

Parton [NAS.CH2/1473] from 1692

Penningham [NAS.CH2/1387] from 1679

Port Glasgow, [NAS.CH2.303] from 1697

Rothesay [NAS.CH2/890] from 1658

Rutherglen [NAS.CH2.315] from 1658

St Boswells [NAS.CH2.313] from 1691

Sorn [NAS.CH2.403] from 1692

Stranraer [NAS.CH2/938] from 1695

Symington [NAS.CH2.728] from 1689

Troqueer [NAS.CH2/1036] from 1698

Wamphrey [NAS.CH2.1530] from 1717

Wiston and Roberton [NAS.CH2.376] from 1689

Yetholm [NAS.CH2.671] from 1691

Synod and Presbytery Records of south-west Scotland also in the National Archives of Scotland:

Presbytery of Ayr [NAS.CH2.532] from 1642

Presbytery of Biggar [NAS.CH2.35] from 1644

Synod of Clydesdale [NAS.CH2.464] from 1687

Presbytery of Dumfries [NAS.CH2.1284] from 1647

Presbytery of Dunbarton, [NAS.CH2.546] from 1639

Presbytery of Dunoon [NAS.CH2.111] from 1639

Synod of Galloway [NAS.CH2.165] from 1664

Presbytery of Glasgow [NAS.CH2.171] from 1592

Presbytery of Hamilton [NAS.CH2.393] from 1687

Presbytery of Jedburgh [NAS.CH2.198] from 1606

Presbytery of Lanark [NAS.CH2.234] from 1623

Synod of Lothian and Tweedale [NAS.CH2.252] from 1589

Presbytery of Paisley, [NAS.CH2.294] from 1602

Presbytery of Selkirk, [NAS.CH2.327] from 1607

Presbytery of Stranraer, [NAS.CH2.341] from 1641

Presbytery of Wigtown, [NAS.CH2.373] from 1696

Very few of the Synod records have been transcribed, edited and published. Among those that have been are the following from which a few typical entries have been extracted:

The Record of the Synod of Lothian and Tweeddale, 1589-1596, 1640-1649, James Kirk, [Edinburgh, 1977].

In November 1641, the assembly was petitioned by the widow and children of the late John Trewman of Ireland who had been murdered for avowing the Scots Covenant. The Synod recommended that the churches within the Synod make a charitable contribution to them.

In November 1642 Thomas Hogg, formerly a minister at Duncannon, County Fermanagh, who, with his wife, children, brothers, and a servant had been forced to flee by the rebels via Mincha Castle and Londonderry to Scotland. Hogg petitioned for support until he was able to return to Ireland.

The Minutes of the Synod of Argyll, 1639-1651, Duncan MacTavish editor [Scottish History Society, Edinburgh, 1943] and **The Minutes of the Synod of Argyll, 1652-1661,** Duncan MacTavish editor [SHS, Edinburgh, 1944] contain a number of Irish references. For example:

At Inveraray on 9 October 1652, Katherine Hamilton in Arran, whose husband had gone to Ireland around 1637 and when she went there enquiring about him discovered that he was dead, having produced a certificate to that effect and he failing to appear before the Synod, she was permitted to re-marry.

At Kilmory, Lorne, on 27 May 1657, Alexander Ross and Isabel Campbell, the children of the same mother, had committed incest in Islay. The resulting child was fostered in Lochaber while the couple fled to "Insck" near Londonderry. A letter was written to the authorities in Ireland requesting that the couple be sent back to appear before the Presbytery of Kintyre.

The Church of Scotland not only had links with the Presbyterian Churches in Ireland from an early date but also with groups of Presbyterians in colonial America. For example, among the Record of the General Assembly of the Church of Scotland is a letter from a congregation of mainly Irish Presbyterians in Newcastle, Pennsylvania, to the General Assembly of the Church of Scotland dated 11 February 1706 [NAS.CH2/28/4].

Biographical data on Presbyterians ministers

Biographical data on the ministers, and their families, of the Church of Scotland from the Reformation of 1560 until modern times are contain in a multi-volumed series entitled *Fasti Ecclesiae Scoticanae,* compiled by Dr Hew Scott, [Oliver & Boyd, Edinburgh, 1915-1928] with later supplements. The data is organised on a Synod, then Presbytery, and finally parish basis. Each parish is described; then follows a chronological list of the parish ministers with much useful genealogical information on them and their families. Some of these ministers moved to Ulster, temporarily or permanently, and occasionally some moved the other way, especially during the seventeenth century. Probably the most relevant volumes to those looking for Irish links are Volume II which deals with the Synods of Merse and Teviotdale, Dumfries and Galloway, Volume III which deals with the Synod of Glasgow and Ayr, and finally Volume VII which has a section dealing with *"ministers connected with the Church of Scotland who have held charges in Ireland since 1613"*. For various reasons certain groups of Presbyterians opted to remain out of the Established Church and formed their own churches. Information on some of these congregations and their preachers can be found in Robert Small's *History of the Congregations of the United Presbyterian Church, 1733-1900,* 2 volumes [D. M. Small, Edinburgh, 1904].

To illustrate the kind of information that can be gleaned from the *Fasti* take the following examples:

Adair, Patrick, son of William Adair minister of Ayr; educated at the University of Glasgow, ordained to Cairncastle on 7 May 1646; removed to Belfast on 13 October 1674; died 1694. He married his cousin, a daughter of Sir Robert Adair of Ballymena, ancestor of Lord Waveney. He left in manuscript "A True Narrative of the Rise and Progress of the Presbyterian Church in Ireland" (edited by W. D. Killen, DD, in 1866) [Fasti.VII.527].

McBride, John, a native of Ireland: graduated Master of Arts at Glasgow University on 15 July 1673; was minister at Clare, Ireland; admitted as minister of the parish of Borgue, Kirk Andrews, and Sennick, in the Presbytery of Kirkcudbright, in 1689; was called to Ayr in 1691, but the Presbytery refused the translation; became a member of the Assembly in 1692. He returned to Ireland and became minister of a church in Belfast on 3 October 1694. He declined the Oath of Abjuration in 1703. Coming back to Glasgow, he preached for a time from 1705 [Fasti.II.396].

Ferguson, Archibald, graduated Master of Arts from St Andrews University in 1642; studied theology at Glasgow University; licensed by the Presbytery of Glasgow on 29 January 1645; ordained about April 1645 as minister of a Presbyterian congregation in Antrim. He was commissioned to the General Assembly in 1649 to ask its influence with the Government for the protection of the Irish Presbyterians. He returned, but with several others was obliged to leave Ireland in 1650 on account of the persecution. He probably was admitted as minister of the parish of Dreghorn in the Presbytery of Irvine about 1652 and died in December 1654, aged around thirty-three years. He married Janet Conyngham, who died in June 1652 [Fasti.III.87].

Monumental Inscriptions

While the Old Parish Registers of the Church of Scotland are invaluable sources of information on births and marriages, they contain virtually nothing on deaths or burials. However, as mentioned earlier the Kirk Session Record do contain information on mortcloth dues, but these are incomplete for the period and naturally only pertain to people buried in the local kirkyard. Gravestone inscriptions, and other such monumental inscriptions, on the other hand, occasionally provide information on people who have gone abroad or have died abroad, including in Ireland. Fortunately for the researcher, it is not necessary to scour the graveyards of south-western Scotland in search of relevant inscriptions as the majority of them have now been transcribed and published. Most of the inscriptions have been collected and published, either on a parish or county basis, by the Scottish Genealogy Society and by local historical and genealogical societies; for example, *The Pre-1855 Gravestone Inscriptions in Carrick, Ayrshire* [SGS, Edinburgh, 1988] and *The Pre-1855 Gravestone Inscriptions of the Stewartry of Kirkcudbright,* two volumes [SGS, Edinburgh, 1990]. A full list of those available appears on the website of the Scottish Genealogy Society. Many gravestones of the seventeenth century are decorated with symbols of mortality, immortality, trade emblems, and heraldic devices. The best guide to these is Betty Willsher's *Understanding Scottish Graveyards* [Canongate, Edinburgh, 1985]. Also of relevance is Thorbjorn Campbell's *Standing Witnesses. A Guide to the Scottish Covenanters and their Memorials with a Historical Introduction* [Saltire Society, Edinburgh, 1996].

The following is an example of the genealogical information obtained from a gravestone in Girvan churchyard:

"Mr Fergus Alexander, minister of the Gospel at Barr who died in February 1689, his age 72, erected by his wife Jean McKerrel in May 1691."

As a minister of the Church of Scotland, he is recorded in the aforementioned *Fasti Ecclesiae Scoticanae*, Volume 3, page 17. According to this source, Fergus Alexander, tutor of Dalreoch, graduated Master of Arts from Glasgow University in 1635, was then minister at Kilmud, Ireland, later minister at Barr from 1653 to 1662 and from 1687 until his death. He married Jean, daughter of William McKerrel of Hillhouse.

The Covenanters

Throughout much of the seventeenth century Presbyterians in Scotland attempted to resist attempts by the Stuart kings to convert the Church of Scotland to an Episcopal church like the Church of England. The religious policy of Charles I led to the outbreak of the Bishop's War in Scotland during 1638, the first of the Wars of the Three Kingdoms which continued until 1651. In 1660 Charles II was restored to the thrones of Scotland and England and soon attempted to reinstate Episcopacy in Scotland. Over 270 ministers in Fife and south western Scotland were ejected from their parishes and soon began to hold illegal conventicles. The government tried to impose a military solution, which led to the Pentland Rising on 1669 that was crushed. Ten years later the Covenanters again rose in armed rebellion against the Stuart government but were heavily defeated at Bothwell Bridge in 1679. Then in 1685 followed the "Killing Time" when government troops summarily executed around 100 men and women mostly of the more militant Presbyterian group known as the Cameronians. All this encouraged many Scottish Presbyterians to take refuge in America, the Netherlands, and Ulster.

Take the case of William Kelso, a 27-year-old surgeon and apothecary from Ayr, who fought as a Covenanter at Bothwell Bridge, and afterwards fled to Ulster before boarding the <u>Anne and Hester</u> bound for Boston in 1680.

In 1683 the ministers of the parishes in Dumfries-shire and Galloway were ordered to compile lists of all residents, male and female, over the age of 12 years, in their parishes. The lists pertaining to the parishes in Wigtownshire for 1684 have been published. They identify 9,276 people in 19 parishes throughout the county. This data was published as *Parish Lists of Wigtownshire and Minnigaff, 1684,* W. Scott [Scottish Record Society, Edinburgh, 1916].

Parish Lists

OF

Wigtownshire and Minnigaff, 1684.

NOTE.—*Names printed in italics are deleted in original.*

A LIST of the Names wt.in the Parishe of GLASTOUN
(GLASSERTON) 15th October 1684.

ARBRICK.
William Donaldsone.
Florence McAdam.
Janet Donaldson.
Jean Donaldson.
Alexr. Hanna.
Jeane Shaw.

COTTARS.
William Bell.
Katharin Houston.
Alexr. McArmick.
Elizabeth Steuart.
Jon. McLockie.
Margrat Robert.
Patrik McAndlish.
Janet Whandle.

AROW.
William McAndlish.
Janet McTutor.
Will. McKechie.
Janet Coning.
Alexr. McKechie.
Jon. McKawin.
Cristian Coning.
Jon. McKawin, yor.
James McKawin.

ARSICK.
Nicol Donan.
Katharin Clanachin.
Jon. Donan.
Agnes Donan.
Jon. Dicksone.
Agnes Malroy.
Agnes Gilkesone.
Janet Crerie.

COTTARS.
Patrik Coltron.
Jean Barthrome.
Jean Clellan.
Jon. Malbratnie.
Janet Hanna.
Elspeth Reid.

KIDDISDAILL.
David Steuart.
Margrat Muir.
Geo. Steuart.
Janet Shank.
Adam McKonnell.
Janet Fie.
Cristian Sloan.
Alexr. Steuart.
Janet Burnie.
Rot. Steuart.
Janet McMillan.
Jon. Ste.

COTTARS.
Andrew Shanke.
Elison Herron.
Geo. Shanke.
James Shanke.
William Steuart.
Margrat Whirter.
Janet Hanna.
Will. Hanna.
Rot. Hanna.
Agnes Hanna.

PHEISGILL.
Jon. Steuart.
Agnes Steuart.
Tho. Steuart.
Agnes Steuart.
Esther Steuart.
Elizabeth Forrest.
Thomas Bairns.
Jean Quibesone.

COTTARS.
William Kinney.
Janet Steuart.
Elspeth Dormant.
Andrew McAndlish.
Janet Keith.
Jon. Steuart.
Margrat Quibesone.

CLAYMODIE.
Rolland McLellan.
Elison McLellan.
Jon. McLellan, yor.
Jon. Livingston.
Margrat McLellan.
Janet Livingston.
Agnes Livingston.
William Hardie.
Janet McNab.
Will. Hardie, yor.
Jean Hardie.
Sarah Hardie.
Margrat Hardie.
Jon. Majorie.
Janet Shankler.
Cristian Coning.

COTTARS.
Janet Bradfoot.
Margrat McLellan.

CHALLOCHBLEWAN.
James Steuart.
Agnes Bardie.
Rot. Steuart.
Agnes Steuart.
Jon. Hanna.
Elspeth Broun.
Grizell Hardie.
Rot. McKie.
Cristian McTutor.
William McKie.
Michael Hanna.
Agnes Dicksone.
Janet Hanna.
Elspeth Hanna

COTTARS.
Jon. McTutor.
Agnes Connell.
Margrat McKie.
Margrat Knox.
Ka. Bradfoot

CHAPTER TWO
Burgh Records

The local government records of the seventeenth century are those of the burghs. Burghs had been increasingly established since the medieval period, mostly as royal burghs established by the king, but also burghs of barony and those of regality founded by the barons and the lords of regality respectively. The royal burghs had more power and importance than the others. While all had commercial rights, only the royal ones could engage in foreign trade.

About forty burghs were semi-autonomous; that is, they had the right to run their own internal affairs. Town councillors were elected from the ranks of the burgesses who represented about 10% of the male adult inhabitants. The right to vote was one of the privileges of a burgess, also was the right to run a business or operate a trade within the burgh. The burgesses were self-sustaining elites, the sons of burgesses could become burgesses, also those who married the daughters of burgesses, and those who had served apprenticeships under existing burgesses. Exceptionally an individual who had performed some outstanding service to the burgh, such as defending the town from attack, was admitted, or someone with vital skills would be made a burgess. In the case of burghs with ports, Scots abroad who might bring economic advantages, such as trading links, might be made burgesses. Finally a small number were purchased their way into the ranks of the burgesses. Latterly town councils conferred honorary burgess-ships on people who had made some major contribution to society at local or national level.

Burgess rolls are clearly of great importance to the family historian as they reveal relationships and occupations. Only a limited number of burgess rolls have been published; many are still in their original manuscript forms, and others may be in typescript in local archives. Formal burgess registers rarely exist and the admittance of new burgesses are noted in multi-purpose burgh court books. Probably the most relevant burgess rolls in print, for Irish connections, is the following: ***The Burgesses and Guild-Brethren of***

Glasgow, 1573-1750, J. R. Anderson [Scottish Record Society, Edinburgh, 1925]. Also among those available are *The Roll of Edinburgh Burgesses and Guild-Brethren, 1406-1700*, C.B. Boog Watson [SRS, Edinburgh, 1929]; *The Roll of Edinburgh Burgesses and Guild-Brethren, 1701-1760*, C.B. Boog Watson [SRS, Edinburgh, 1930]; *The Roll of Dumbarton Burgesses and Guild-Brethren, 1600-1846*, F. Roberts [SRS, Edinburgh, 1937] and *The Burgesses and Guild Brethren of Ayr, 1647 to 1846*, A. Lindsay and J. Kennedy [Ayrshire Federation of Historical Societies, Ayr, 2002].

[573-1750] *Burgesses and Guild Brethren of Glasgow.* 103

1640.

Adam, James, merchant, B., by purchase (G.B., as mar. Helen, l. dau.
    to dec. William Weimes, merchant, B. and G.B., 17 June 1658)   17 Dec.
Peter, David, merchant, B. and G.B., as mar. Bessie, l. dau. to dec.
    Walter Lochhead, baxter, B. and G.B.   17 Dec.
Pettigrew, John, maltman, B., as second l. son to Thomas P.,
    maltman, burgess   31 Dec.
Kerr, Robert, merchant, B. and G.B., by purchase   31 Dec.

1641.

Campbell, James, merchant, B. and G.B., as mar. Margaret, l. dau. to
    Archibald Lowk, maltman, B. and G.B.   7 Jan.
Paterson, John, weaver, B. and G.B., as eld. l. son to dec. John P.,
    weaver, B. and G.B.   14 Jan.
Wright, Michael, clothier, B., by purchase[1]   14 Jan.
Rowane, William, tailor, B., by purchase   14 Jan.
Barr, John, skinner, B. and G.B., as eld. l. son to Patrick B., skinner,
    B. and G.B.   14 Jan.
Wilson, Matthew, tanner, B. and G.B., as second l. son to John W.,
    cordiner, B. and G.B.   14 Jan.
Smalie, William, maltman, B. and G.B., as mar. Helen, l. dau. to dec.
    John Young, cooper, B. and G.B.   14 Jan.
Clark, William, weaver, B., as eld. l. son to Patrick C., weaver,
    burgess (G.B., by same right, 17 June 1658)   28 Jan.
Scott, John, armourer, B., by right of his apprenticeship (G.B., by
    same right, 6 April 1648)   28 Jan.
Gibson, John, weaver, B., as mar. Jonat, l. dau. to Matthew Dorroche,
    smith, burgess   4 Feb.
Lang, Robert, weaver, B. and G.B., as eld. l. son to Patrick L.,
    weaver, B. and G.B.   11 Feb.
Jamesone, John, weaver, B., as eld. l. son to Robert J., chyrurgane,
    burgess (G.B., as serving appr. with Archibald Glen, weaver,
    19 April 1666)   11 Feb.
Robesoun, John, tailor, B. as mar. [——], l. dau. to dec. [——]
    Greinleis, cordiner, burgess   11 Feb.
Paterson, John, cooper, B., as serving appr. with Daniel Anderson,
    cooper   11 Feb.
Parkhill, James, skinner, B., as serving appr. with Henry Smith,
    skinner   11 Feb.
King, John, weaver, B., as mar. [——], l. dau. to Malcolm Bankeir,
    maltman, burgess[2]   11 Feb.
Brown, Robert, flesher, B. and G.B., as second l. son to George B.,
    elder, flesher, B. and G.B.   25 Feb.
Walker, John, hammerman, B. and G.B., as eld. l. son to dec. John
    W., hammerman, B. and G.B.   25 Feb.
Rankein, James, maltman, B. and G.B., as mar. Agnes, l. dau. to dec.
    John Mudie, B. and G.B.   25 Feb.
Lowk, John, merchant, B. and G.B., as eld. l. son to Archibald L.,
    maltman, B. and G.B.   25 Feb.
Moresoun, Andrew, weaver, B., as mar. Jonat, l. dau. to dec. John
    Stewart, fisher, burgess   25 Feb.
Bowman, William, weaver [son to William B. in Rutherglen[3]], B., as
    serving appr. with George Paterson, younger, weaver, and others   25 Feb.
Watson, James, younger, tailor, B. (G.B., by purchase, 31 August 1643)   25 Feb.
Kyll, John, cordiner, B., as eld. l. son to dec. Robert K., cordiner,
    burgess   25 Feb.

[1] Having removed from Glasgow and settled in Tranent, he was deprived of his
freedom by act of council 18 Aug. 1655.
[2] Having removed from Glasgow and settled in Ireland, he was deprived of his
freedom by act of council 18 Aug. 1655.
[3] *Rec. Trades Ho.*, p. 150.

Burgesses were expected to live within the burgh and play their fair share in supporting the town, for example, by defending the town if necessary. According to the published Burgess Roll of Glasgow, Robert Craig who was admitted as a maltman burgess of Glasgow on 2 August 1649 by right of his wife Jean, daughter of Archibald Sempill a maltman burgess and guildsbrother, was deprived of his rights as a burgess when he left the burgh and moved to Ireland in 1655. This was not a unique event. Allan Cuthbert, a merchant, who had been admitted as a burgess and guilds-brother of Glasgow, being the eldest son of John Cuthbert a fisher burgess and guilds-brother of Glasgow, on 17 February 1642, also was stripped of his burgess rights in 1655 when he left Glasgow and settled in Ireland.

The records of these burghs are generally to be found in local hands, sometimes still in the hands of the burghs but increasingly in local archives. For example the University of St Andrews' library Department of Special Collections holds all the burgh records of the district of North East Fife, while the Ayr Archives contain substantial local records.

Records of the burghs lying south-west of a line from Glasgow to Dumfries would be the most likely sources of reference to Scots in Ulster. However, some other burghs also contain relevant source material. For example, Edinburgh City Archives contains a mass of unpublished material some of which is termed "the Moses Bundles," which has links with Ireland. On 18 September 1667, Robert Jeffes, a merchant burgess of Edinburgh, then in Birr, King's County, Ireland, disposed of property to Thomas Porteous, a merchant burgess, and his wife Janet Wardroper. On 11 August 1625 John Mitchelhill, a minister at Balliphillip, Ireland, son of John Mitchelhill, a merchant burgess of Edinburgh, and the late Barbara Gilchrist, disposed of property in Edinburgh. Such information leads on to other sources within the town's records. The published burgess records of Edinburgh reveal that a John Mitchelhill was admitted as a burgess and guilds-brother on 9 January 1579 by right of his wife Euphame, eldest daughter of Robert Gray a merchant burgess, [sic!].

Any property within the burgh will be identifiable through the burgh's registers of sasines. John Mitchelhill being a minister is likely to have been educated at university, in this case probably Edinburgh, so the university matriculation rolls should also be consulted.

Every burgh had the right of internal self-government and maintained records such as the burgh court book. Many of these, and similar records of the period, have survived and can be invaluable to the genealogical researcher. Most, however, remain in manuscript form, which probably will cause problems for most researchers. The sort of material that may be found can be illustrated through the following example:

The Kirkcudbright Burgh Court Book of 11 May 1642 records the fact that Robert Lig, the burgh drummer, had enrolled as drummer of Captain William McClellan's company of foot soldiers bound for Ireland, despite his existing contract with the burgh. The town council found him guilty of breaking his existing contract and his father Stephen Lig guilty of encouraging him. Robert was to be put in the stocks until sunset and thereafter jailed, while his parents were banished from Kirkcudbright. Elsewhere in the Burgh Court Book there is a reference to Margaret McClellan, sister of Lord Kirkcudbright, bound for Ireland in May 1656.

Books of this type include *The Court Book of Kirkintilloch, 1658-1694,* G.S.Pryde [Scottish History Society, Edinburgh, 1963]; *Dumbarton Common Good Accounts, 1614-1660,* F. Roberts and I. M. M. MacPhail [Dumbarton Town Council, Dumbarton, 1972]; and *The Lochmaben Court and Council Book, 1612-1721,* J.B. Wilson [Scottish Record Society, Edinburgh, 2001].

The Registers of Sasines of the Royal Burghs

All the forty or so royal burghs maintained their own internal registers of sasines which recorded the transfer of ownership of property within the burgh boundaries. The royal burghs in the south-west which are in the National Archives of Scotland include Ayr from 1700, Dumbarton from 1681, Dumfries from 1668, Irvine from 1721, Jedburgh from 1707, Kirkcudbright from 1681, Lanark from 1616, Renfrew from 1738, Rothesay from 1671, Rutherglen from 1692, Sanquhar from 1718, Stranraer from 1683, Whithorn from 1684, and Wigtown from 1724. Those of Glasgow can be found in the Glasgow Archives.

Registers of Apprentices

The training of apprentices by existing merchants and craftsmen, all burgesses and guild-brothers, was formally recorded in the burgh and trade records. Apprentices were required to serve under a master for several years before qualifying; the period varied from trade to trade and over time but could last up to seven years. Thereafter they became journeymen and worked for master craftsmen. After a period they were eligible to establish their own firms but firstly had to be admitted as burgesses, and later as guild brothers if they became merchants. The right to become a burgess has been discussed elsewhere in this book but one of the routes available was by having served an apprenticeship under an existing burgess of the burgh. Therefore records of apprenticeships were carefully kept. Very few of such records have been published, but without doubt the single most important Register of Apprentices was that of Edinburgh which has been published for the period 1583 to 1666, from 1666 to 1700, and also 1701 to 1755, which roughly coincides with the period of this book. Edinburgh, the largest and most important city in Scotland, had a population of around 50,000 in the seventeenth century. It attracted immigrants from all over Scotland and elsewhere to a lesser extent. Some of these came on a temporary basis, for education at Edinburgh University or to serve apprenticeships. A number of young men arrived from Ireland for this purpose as is shown in the Register of Apprentices; for example, James Jardine, son of William Jardine in Coleraine, was indentured as an apprentice to John Leyne, merchant in Edinburgh, on 21 November 1649; while Thomas Kennedy, son of the late David Kennedy of

Killrenie in Ireland, was indentured as an apprentice to John McLurge, a merchant in Edinburgh, on 2 November 1655. See *The Register of Apprentices of the City of Edinburgh, 1583-1666*, F.J.Grant [Scottish Record Society, Edinburgh, 1906]; *The Register of Edinburgh Apprentices, 1666-1700*, C.B.Boog-Watson [SRS, Edinburgh, 1929]; and *The Register of Edinburgh Apprentices, 1701-1755*, C.B.Boog-Watson [SRS, Edinburgh, 1929].

Register of Edinburgh Apprentices, 1666-1700.

Abercrombie, Alexr., s. to Thomas A., p. to James Wilsone, younger, mt.   13 June 1666
  „ James, s. to late Thomas A. in Leith, p. to Patrick Wat, mt.   13 Apr. 1670
  „ Patrick, s. to dec. Sir Alexr. A. of Birnboig, p. to James Nicolson of Trabrown, mt. (B.)   6 June 1694
Adam, George, s. to dec. John A., fermorer at Inglistoun, p. to Richard Brown, candlemaker (B.)   19 Apr. 1700
  „ Wm., s. to Wm. A., elder, mt. in Cullros, p. to John Cairns, stationer   27 Oct. 1680
  „ Wm., s. to dec. George A., tailor, p. to Andrew Powrie, apothecary (B.)   12 Jan. 1687
Adamson, Alexr., s. to Andrew A., indweller, p. to Archd. Hamiltoun, mt.   21 Apr. 1686
  „ Francis, s. to dec. James A. of Fleures, p. to John Armour, tailor (B.)   29 Mar. 1699
  „ James, s. to James A., customer at the west port, p. to James Padyeane, writer   29 Oct. 1673
  „ James, s. to umq. Andrew A., fermourer, in Fordellmylne, p. to John Campbell, yor., tanner   1 Apr. 1685
  „ John, s. to Walter A. in Dalkeith, p. to John Adamson, baxter   28 Feb. 1666
  „ John, s. to Mr. John A., minr. of the gospel, p. to James Reid, mt.   9 July 1679
  „ John, s. to dec. James A., indweller, p. to Androw Nisbet, candlemaker   5 Sept. 1683
  „ John, s. to Alexr. A., indweller, p. to James Lenie, skinner   11 May 1687
  „ Patrick, s. to Patrick A., tenant to Alexr. Brand of Barbertoun, p. to John Lawder, coppersmith (B.)   13 Nov. 1695
  „ Robert, s. to Andrew A. in Fordellmill, p. to James Adamson, baxter. (*Deleit of consent*)   18 Aug. 1669
Adinston (Admiston), Lawrance, s. to Thomas A. of Kirkcant, p. to John Nasmyth, wright   6 June 1688
  „ Wm., s. to Thomas A. of Carcant (Kirkcant), p. to Gavin Drysdaill, baxter   3 June 1674
Agnew, Alexr., s. to Alexr. A., indweller in Ireland, p. to Robert Selkirk, mt.   27 Aug. 1679
  „ Thomas, second s. to Sir Andrew A. of Lochnaw, p. to Robert Blackwood, mt.   23 Feb. 1687
Aikfurd, Robert, s. to late Thomas A. in Wormistoun, p. to John Loch, mt.   27 May 1674
Aikman, Andrew, s. to James A. in Williamston, p. to Robert Somervaill, skinner (B.)   6 Nov. 1696
  „ John, s. to John A. in Woodhouse of Calder, p. to Samuel Purdy, skinner   11 May 1681
  „ Wm., s. to John A. in the paroch of Crawmond, p. to John Shaw, baxter (B.)   1 Nov. 1693
Ainslie, Adam, s. to Wm. A., indweller, p. to John Blaiky, hatmaker   22 Aug. 1683

A

Craft and Trade Guilds

From the medieval period onwards the craftsmen or tradesmen and merchants of the burghs each had their own society. These societies or guilds were committed to establishing and maintaining standards, protecting the rights of their members, supervising the training of apprentices, and ensuring that only members of the guild operated within the burgh boundaries. By 1600 Glasgow had fourteen incorporated trades, such as the Incorporation of Hammermen which included all sorts of metal-workers – blacksmiths, goldsmiths, lorimers, saddlers, bucklemakers, armorers, and others. The members of the craft and trades guilds were all burgesses, either as craftsmen or merchants. Numerically they amounted to nearly 10 per cent of the male adults in the average burgh, but had all the social and economic advantages available. The bulk of the burgh population were "unfreemen" who formed the under-privileged poor who left few records. Any Scottish settler in seventeenth century Ulster who arrived as a trained merchant or qualified craftsman would have been recorded within the craft or guild records of one of the Scottish burghs where they exist. A few have been published such as *The History of the Hammermen of Glasgow,* H. Lumsden and P. H. Aitken [Paisley, 1912] which includes a list of member from 1616 to 1733 and from 1775 to 1911. Others are still in their original manuscript form, some in local or national archives, while others still in the hands of the guilds. Among those held in the NAS are the fleshers of Ayr, 1661-1891 [NAS.E870.6]; the weavers of Ayr, 1657-1849 [NAS.E870.5]; the bonnetmakers of Stewarton, 1673-1790 [NAS.GD1.300]; and the goldsmiths of Glasgow, 1525-1964 [NAS.GD1.482].

CHAPTER THREE
Court Records

There are various courts throughout Scotland, though mainly in Edinburgh, that contain data of relevance to family historians.

The Court of Session is the highest civil court in Scotland. Its massive collection of documents cover a period of four hundred and fifty years and are partly catalogued in a NAS guide entitled *Court of Session Processes after 1660.* One of the most important of the court's records is its Register of Deeds.

The Registers of Deeds, both of the Court of Session and those of the Burghs, contain a wide range of documentation, such as dispositions, marriage contracts, apprenticeship records, and commercial documents such as bills of exchange, to name but a few.

These Registers of Deeds of the Court of Session, now in the NAS, date from the mid-sixteenth century and continue to the present day. The first series cover the period 1554 to 1657, the second dates from 1661 to 1811, and the third brings us up to date. Clearly on a chronological basis the first two series are likely to contain data of relevance. However, the early deeds are likely to cause palaeographic problems to most researchers, and there are no transcriptions available. The first series is partly indexed for much of the period up to 1595, while the second series is indexed from 1661 to 1715 and from 1750 onwards. Examples include the following:

On 15 December 1617 Sir Robert McClellan of Bombie received 720 merks from Thomas Kelso in Bellchachanner, County Down, in exchange for 300 acres in the "Clothiers proportion". Deed registered on 6 December 1620 [NAS.RD1.301].

Thomas McClellan of Mullochmoir gave a bond to James Hamilton of Ballychemagry, County Tyrone, in 1619, which was witnessed by Thomas McClellan of Straby. The deed was registered on 21 March 1621 [NAS.RD1.304].

Source: Books of Council and Session, Register of Deeds, Volume 615, 13 December 1655. Contract, dated at Irvine 2 November 1647, between Hew Campbell of Dowcathall, with consent of Hew Campbell, apparent thereof, his eldest son, now being of the age of 21 years complete, on the one part, and Martha Pont, widow of Mr Josias Welshe, minister at Temple Patrick in the county of Antrim, Ireland, and Mr John, Margaret and Loaz Welshe her three lawful children, on the other part, whereby for 2400 merks paid by the said Martha she and her children are to be infeft in the 5 merklands of Boigend and Ardeires in the parish of Stevenson [NAS.RD1.615].

Source: Books of Council and Session, Register of Deeds, Volume 494, 29 June 1636. Discharge by Captain William Campbell, brother german to Colin Campbell of Balleherring in Ireland, to Annas Colquhoun, widow of Colin Campbell, fiar of Carrick, and Archibald Campbell, brother german of the said deceased Colin Campbell, for 2500 merks due to him as tocher with Margaret Campbell, second lawful daughter of the said deceased Colin, conform to their Contract of Marriage, dated at Rosenkill in Ireland and Cammindaill in Rosneith in Scotland 29 September 1634 and 18 April 1635 respectively. The discharge is dated at Rothesay 13 January 1636 and is witnessed by John Campbell, provost of Rothesay, and Duncan Campbell, brother of the Captain of Dunoon, and written by George Campbell, sheriff clerk of Argyll [NAS.RD1.494].

Source: as above, Volume 544, 3 December 1642. Discharge by John Maxwell (lege Campbell), brother german of the deceased James Campbell of Arbuikle, to William Friar, merchant burgess of....for all accounts standing between them, dated at Carrickfergus 14 November 1642 [NAS.RD1.544].

Protest regarding an unpaid bill of exchange for £50 sterling issued in Dumfries on 8 February 1715 in favour of Reverend James Pearson at Killibeggs, County Donegal, endorsed in favour of Mr Isaac McKertney a merchant in Belfast. Reference to George Carrick, John Humphrey, James Downey, and Alexander Stewart [NAS.RD2.105.77].

Sheriff Court Records

Since the twelfth century sheriffs have represented the Crown as judge and administrator, and the sheriffdom has been an important unit of government. Their accounts, dating from the medieval period, are to be found in the National Archives of Scotland. Those of the seventeenth century are in their original manuscript form. Records dating from before the Union of Parliaments in 1707 are referenced NAS.E38, while those after that date are listed under NAS.E236. The more likely ones to contain links to Ireland are the following:

Sheriffdom of Argyll, at Inveraray 1605-1908 [NAS.SC54]; at Tobermory 1635-1936 [NAS.SC59]; and at Dunoon 1664-1977 [SC51]

Sheriffdom of Ayr, at Ayr 1503-1981 [NAS.SC6]

Sheriffdom of Dumfries at Dumfries 1537-1991 [NAS.SC15]

Sheriffdom of Dumbarton at Dumbarton 1682-1981 [NAS.SC65]

Sheriffdom of Kirkcudbright at Kirkcudbright 1623-1976 [NAS.SC16]

Sheriffdom of Lanark at Hamilton 1548-1981 [NAS.SC37]; Lanark 1607-1968 [NAS.SC38]; at Glasgow [NAS.SC36]

Sheriffdom of Renfrew at Paisley 1618-1980 [NAS.SC58]

Sheriffdom of Wigtown at Wigtown 1629-1975

Another potential source within the Sheriff Court Record are the Registers of Deeds. These can be substantial. Take the case of Kirkcudbright Sheriff Court, which has 28 volumes of deeds for the seventeenth century alone, see NAS.SC16.56.1-28. Registers of Deeds contain a wide range of manuscripts; for example, among the entries in the Argyll Sheriff Court Book, Volume 6, of 4 March 1720 is the marriage contract of Alexander Stewart, a saddler in Coleraine, and Isobel, daughter of Duncan Campbell of Elister in Argyll, dated 18 June 1706. The deed also refers to her brothers George, Colin, John, and Alexander Campbell.

Registers of Testaments

From the Reformation of 1560 right up until the early nineteenth century, Scots had their wills confirmed by Commissary Courts; thereafter Sheriff Courts took over this function. However, within the period being considered, it was the Commissary Courts that were used for this purpose. A testament can be either "testate," that is, a will exists and an executor or executors have been appointed (a testament testamentary), or "intestate," when the deceased has not left a will and where the court appoints an executor or executors, (a testament dative). The Commissary Courts were based on the dioceses of the pre-Reformation Roman Catholic Church; later the Commissariat of Edinburgh was established. The Commissary of Edinburgh could be used by Scots resident anywhere in Scotland or by Scots abroad including Ireland. Many Scots living abroad opted to have their wills proved in the Prerogative Court of Canterbury or locally where a colonial probate office existed. Wills can also be found in court records and registers of deeds in Scotland; some may even be found among family papers. The Registers of Testaments can now be accessed via the website www.scottishdocuments.com

The Commissary Court records, which are all in the National Archives of Scotland, contain more than just testaments. The Commissary Courts which are most likely to contain material of relevance to Ulster Scots are those of Dumfries, [NAS.CC5], Edinburgh, [NAS.CC8], Glasgow, [NAS.CC9], Kirkcudbright, [NAS.CC13], Lanark, [NAS.CC14], and Wigtown, [NAS.CC22]. All the pre-1800 testaments that have survived were indexed, and these were published in Edinburgh by the Scottish Record Society between 1897 and 1904. These comprise Glasgow, 1547 to 1800; Dunblane, 1539-1800; Argyle, 1674-1800; The Isles, 1661 to 1800; Peebles, 1681-1699; Brechin, 1576-1800; Dumfries, 1624 to 1800; St Andrews, 1549 to 1800; Inverness, 1630 to 1800; Hamilton and Campsie; 1564 to 1800; Aberdeen, 1715 to 1800; Caithness, 1661 to 1664; Dunkeld, 1682 to 1800; Kirkcudbright, 1663 to 1800; Lauder, 1561 to 1800; Lanark, 1595-1800; Moray, 1684-1800; Orkney and Shetland, 1611 to 1684; Stirling, 1607 to 1800; Wigtown, 1700 to 1800; and Edinburgh, 1514 to 1800. Since publication, a number of omissions have been discovered, and accordingly the indexes in the NAS have been updated.

| 176 | *Commissariot of Edinburgh.* | [1701-1800. |

M'Kinnon, Neill, barber and wigmaker in Edinburgh, thereafter drover at Glenegies		13 Mar. 1753
Maclachlan or **Maclauchlan,** Alexander, writer in Edinburgh		9 Feb. 1793
„ Lieutenant Alexander. *See* **Farquharson,** Isobel.		
„ Archibald, sailor or mariner aboard the ship "Defiance," man-of-war		25 Nov. 1721
„ Archibald, merchant in Edinburgh		29 Mar. 1748
„ Mr. Daniel, late minister at Ardnamurchan		16 May 1745
„ Henry, merchant in Belfast, Ireland		25 Mar. 1743
„ John, musitioner in Edinburgh		30 July 1702
„ Lauchlan, master of the sloop "Glengarry" of Fort William		9 Feb. 1793
„ Lauchlane, sometime soldier in the town-guard of Edinburgh		10 Aug. 1708
M'Lagan, Ensign Alexander, of Lord Loudoun's Regiment		19 Aug. 1746
„ John, writer in Edinburgh		15 Apr. 1761
Maclaren, Alexander, brewer in Leith		16 June 1770
„ Daniel, turner in Edinburgh		31 Aug. 1789
„ David, merchant in Leith	16 Jan. 1789 and	15 June 1793
„ Duncan, coppersmith in Edinburgh		1 June 1752
„ James, gardener at the Foot of Leith Walk		14 Nov. 1781
„ John, sailor in Perth		25 Feb. 1793
„ Katrine, relict of William M'Donald, soldier in Stirling Castle		11 Jan. 1724
„ Mary, relict of Alexander Thomson, journeyman weaver in Portsburgh		24 May 1749
„ Thomas, indweller in Leith. *See* **Claret,** Thomas.		
M'Lary, Robert, late servant to Robert Wood of Brumpton		17 June 1767
M'Laurin, John, of Dreghorn, senator of the College of Justice		26 May 1797
M'Lea, Mr. Duncan, minister of Innerchillan		23 Nov. 1785
Maclean, Sir Alexander, of Otter, sometime commissarie of Argyle, and son lawful to the deceased Hector, sometime Bishop of Argyle	14 May 1714 and	20 Aug. 1726
„ Andrew, late lint-dresser in Edinburgh		27 Mar. 1797
„ Archibald, linen-draper in London		10 Dec. 1765
„ Archibald, merchant in London		25 Apr. 1772
„ Charles, in America, sailor, of Glasgow		26 Dec. 1795
„ Daniel, steward's mate aboard the ship "Rising Sun"		3 Oct. 1707
„ Donald, merchant in Kersie		15 June 1780
„ Donald, planter and merchant at St. Augustine in East Florida, North America		25 Jan. 1786
„ George, merchant in Cawnpore, in the East Indies		25 Nov. 1796
„ Hector, writer in Edinburgh		30 Aug. 1765
„ Hugh, late servant to Lord Blantyre		13 June 1745
„ Lieut. John, of the Earl of Portmore's Regiment of Foot, and son to umquhile Hector, Bishop of Argyle		14 Mar. 1711
„ John, lawful son to the deceased Hector, Bishop of Argyle, and Helen Forbes, his relict, lawful daughter to the deceased Mr. Duncan F., of Ugstoun		27 July 1717
„ Captain John, of Colonel Wolff's Regiment of Marines		3 July 1741
„ John, merchant in Edinburgh		24 Nov. 1772
„ John, Lieutenant in the 2d Battalion of the Royal Highland Emigrants, commanded by Gen. Sir Henry Clinton		31 May 1783
„ Lachlan, vintner at Fountainbridge. par. of St. Cuthbert		1 July 1755
„ Lauchland, of Strontian		29 July 1768
„ Margaret, residenter in Edinburgh, daughter to the deceased Ewan M'L., son to the Laird of Borary		16 Jan. 1741
„ Murdoch, of Lochbuy		19 Apr. 1727
„ Captain Murdoch, of Colonel Myres' West India Regiment		6 Jan. 1797
„ William, master of the Revells in Edinburgh		10 July 1718
„ William, merchant in North Leith. *See* **Wood,** Anna.		

Among those with links to Ireland is the testament of Henry McLachlan merchant in Belfast, which was confirmed with the Commissariat of Edinburgh in 1743, [NAS.CC8.8.107-178], of which the following is an abstract:

Testament dative and inventory of the debts and sums of money pertaining and adebted to the umquhill Henry McLachlan, merchant in Belfast in the Kingdom of Ireland, at the time of his decease who died in 1741. Faithfully made and given up by Duncan Fisher, writer in Inverary, as factor for and in the name and for the behoof of Elizabeth McLachlan and her husband James Henderson merchant in Belfast, Ireland, Elizabeth being sister german to the said umquhill Henry McLachlan his only executrix dative.

Another is the testament of Robert Byers, a merchant in Dublin, who died abroad. Made and given up by Patrick Byers of Fouley, Aberdeenshire, his son and only executor dative appointed by the Commissary of Edinburgh on 21 June 1735. Assets in the form of furniture and plenishings were valued at £100 Scots. Cautioner – James Moir, a writer in Edinburgh, son of Alexander Moir, Professor of Philosophy in Edinburgh. Confirmed on 2 January 1735 [NAS.CC8.8.103].

Testament dative and inventory of Isobell Allan, daughter of the deceased James Allan a merchant in Belfast, who died in Edinburgh. Made and given up by Colin Robertson, wigmaker in Edinburgh, son of John Robertson a merchant in Edinburgh, procreated between him and the late Rachaell Allan his spouse, who was sister german of the said deceased James Allan father to the deceased, which Colin Robertson, cousin-german to the umquhill Isobell Allan, is the only executor dative as decreed by the Commissary of Edinburgh on 8 April 1741. At the time of her death Isabell Allan had a bed, a striped gown, and a blue coat, also eight gold guineas, with a total value of £9.2 shillings, now in the hands of Elizabeth Blair, wife of George Watters, a preacher and justice of the peace for Edinburgh. Less funeral expenses, the net value was £8.9 shillings [NAS.CC8.8.104].

Extracts of testaments in the Record of the Commissariot of Glasgow from 1547 to 1659 form an appendix to the *Topographical Account of the district of Cunningham, Ayrshire* written by Timothy Pont and published in Glasgow in 1858.

Some of these contain links to nearby Ireland, as shown in the following abstracts:

"Testament etc. of Johne Montgomerie of Cockilbie, Stewartone, who deceased November 1638, and who appears to have been possessed of the lands of Braidstone at his period. Legacie:- At Cockinblie, the xix day of August 1636 yeiris, etc., the quhilk day, I Johne Montgomerie of Cockilbie, nominates Jeane Forrester, my wife, my onlie executrix, and leivis hir tutrix to my children, Johne, Agnes, Barbara, Margaret, and Katherine Montgomeries. And failzeing of hir, I leive William Montgomerie of Brigend, William Shaw provost, and William Cauldwell of that Ilk, tutouris to my saidis childrein. [They are to be accountable "unto Sir James Montgomerie of Gray Abbey, Neill Montgomerie" of Langschaw, and Mr William Castlelaw, minister of Stewartone"]. He likewise gives full power to William Schaw, foresaid, to sett, raise, output and input tenantis in my landis of Ballibuttle and Killivogane [doubtless in Ireland]. The will is written in his own hand, at Cockilbie, the last day of August 1636, and was confirmed on 11 March 1648. David Montgomerie, now of Cockilbie, appearing as cautioner for the executrix, his mother."

The following distinct traces of emigration from Ayrshire in the early part of the seventeenth century occur in this testament:

"Jonet Archibald, spous to Johne Huid, in Kirktoun of Lairgs," – as debtore "item, be Johne Erskyne, now duelland at the heid of Lochsullie; item, be Petir Barclay, now duelland within Strangfuird, or thereby in Ireland; item, be Archibald Thomesoun, now duelland within the countrie of Clannybowie, in Ireland; item, be James Miller, cowper, now in the Airdis of Ireland, etc. Confirmed on March 23, 1630."

Many similar notices respecting this part of the country appear in these and other local records.

As an example of what records these contain, take the Commissariat of Dumfries which has the following:

Act Books, 1656-1828. [NAS.CC5.1]; decrees, 1663-1747. [NAS.CC5.2-3]; processes, 1675-1704, 1711, 1716-1823, [NAS.CC5.4]; and court Record, 1665-1813 [NAS.CC5.5]
Register of Testaments, 1624-1827 [NAS.CC5.6]
Minute Book of Testaments, 1694-1715 [NAS.CC5.7]
Warrants of Testaments and Wills, 1694-1829 [NAS.CC5.8]
Warrants of Inventories, 1741-1830 [NAS.CC5.10]
Petitions, 1714-1829 [NAS.CC5.11]
Edicts of Executry, 1704-1828 [NAS.CC5.12]
Acts and Bonds of Caution, 1673-1830 [NAS.CC5.13/14]
Deeds and Probative Writs, 1650-1809 [NAS.CC5.15/19]
Inventories, 1685-1813 [NAS.CC5.21]

Since the Reformation of 1560, divorce has been possible in Scotland. Until 1830 the Commissariat of Edinburgh was responsible for the constitution and dissolution of marriages. The Record of this have been abstracted and published under the title *The Commissariat of Edinburgh: Consistorial Processes and Decreets, 1658-1800* [Scottish Record Society, Edinburgh, 1909]. These too contain items of interest for those searching their Scots-Irish roots as well as Scottish roots. The illustrations below record a Process of Divorce of Captain James Marshall from County Fermanagh and his wife Ann, daughter of Sir Robert Montgomery of Skelmorlie in Ayrshire, who had married in Edinburgh in 1692, and also a declaration that a marriage had occurred between Christopher Irving and Margaret Wishart in Ireland in 1639, which had been made to establish the right of succession.

50. **Process of Scandal**—Robert Bull, wright, burgess of Edinburgh, against George Porteous, herald painter, Edinburgh   1690
51. **Process of Divorce on Impotency**—Marion Miller, daughter to John Miller in Barshalloch, parish of Cardross, against John Reid, indweller in said parish. No warrants
                                              I 30   14 Nov. 1690
52 **Process of Divorce**—John Kerr, merchant, burgess of Edinburgh, against Cecil Scott, lawful daughter to Francis Scott, late keeper of the minute book, his spouse, married 25 September 1690, at which time the pursuer alleged she was with child to John Leslie, writer in Edinburgh, which was born on 1st January 1691, a son   I 49   8 July 1691
53. **Process of Scandal**—Hugh Walker in Burnbrae, against George Sheill in Sheill Milne   1691
54. **Process of Scandal**—Edward Burd of Foord, against James Justice of Easter Crichton   1691
55. **Supplication**—Sophia Drummond, daughter to Sir William Drummond of Hawthornden, anent her pretended marriage with John Murray of Cringlety   I 37   3 Apr. 1691
56. **Process of Divorce for Impotency**—The same against the same, married at Holyroodhouse, 4 Apr. 1678.   No warrants
                                              I 39   27 June 1691
57. **Process of Divorce**—Colonel George Lauder of Ravelrig, against Elizabeth Williamina Van Ghent, his spouse, married at the church of Huriewynie, in Bommelerwert in Gelderland, in April 1682 ; Sergeant M'Ghie, co-respondent. No warrants   I 91   27 Feb. 1692
58. **Process of Scandal**—Robert Row, brewer, burgess of Edinburgh, against John Tweedie, brewer in Edinburgh   1692
59. **Process of Scandal**—Andrew Hepburn, burgess of North Berwick, against John Home and Archibald Lauder, burgesses of North Berwick, and George Simpson, clerk thereof
                                                                    1693
60. **Process of Divorce**—Anna Montgomery, second lawful daughter to umquhile Sir Robert Montgomery of Skelmorlie, against Captain James Marshall, late merchant in Newportoun in county of Fermanagh, in the kingdom of Ireland, her spouse, married February 1692, at Edinburgh
                                              I 115   2 Feb. 1693
61. **Process of Divorce on Impotency**—Janet Nickcalm, *alias* M'Gillairint, lawful daughter to Donald Mackcalm in Polacherorkoran, parish of Lochgoilhead, against Patrick M'Glass, son to the deceased John M'Glass, residing in Euronich, and said parish of Lochgoilhead, married Feb. 1677, at Lochgoylhead church   I 128   14 Nov. 1693
62. **Process of Divorce on Impotency**—Janet Mackmaluach, lawful daughter to the deceased Donald Mackmaluach in Glencroe, parish of Lochgoylhead, against Archibald M'Glassan, son to Duncan M'Glassan, tenant in Strachur, married January 1686 at Strachur church I 121   14 Nov. 1693
63. **Process of Scandal**—John Binning, merchant in Edinburgh, against John Thomson, merchant tailor in Edinburgh   1693
64. **Process of Adherence**—Elizabeth Heriot, lawful daughter to the deceased Captain Archibald Heriot, sometime residenter in Edinburgh, against Alexander Tennant, merchant in Edinburgh, her spouse, married in Old Church of Edinburgh   I 132   14 Dec. 1694
65. **Process of Divorce**—Lady Margaret Mackenzie, eldest lawful daughter to George, Lord Viscount of Tarbet, against David Bruce of Clackmannan, her spouse, married July 1674, at West Kirk of Edinburgh   I 139   21 Aug. 1694

66. **Process of Declarator of Marriage, &c.**—Mr. Christopher Irving of Castle Irving in Ireland, doctor of medicine, only child in life of deceased Mr. Christopher Irving, doctor of medicine and residenter in Edinburgh, and of the deceased Mrs Margaret Wishart, daughter to the deceased James Wishart of Pittarrow, his spouse, against Elizabeth Ker, indweller in Edinburgh, John Irving, son to the deceased Mr. Christopher Irvine, Sidney Carleton, relict of the deceased Thomas Irvine, indweller in Edinburgh, and . . . Irvine, their daughter, and the tutors and curators of the said John and . . . Irvings. Christopher Irving and Margaret Wishart, married in Ireland in 1639, and had issue three children, Christopher and James and Gerard, bapt. at South Leith, 3 Feb. 1650. Thomas Irving, now deceased, and said John Irving, born in adultery of said Dr. Christopher, deceased, with Jean Kerr. Margaret Wishart returned to Ireland and died there, Feb. 1689. Sir Gerard Irving of Castle Irving, brother to said Dr. Christopher. Declarator that pursuer is the only heir of said Dr. Christopher   I 155   6 Aug. 1695

67. **Process of Scandal**—John Alves, writer in Edinburgh, against John Clerk, writer in Edinburgh, ordinarily called Hamilton John Clerk   1694

68. **Process of Adherence**—Thomas Symmers, flesher in Edinburgh, against Jean Boyd, daughter to the deceased Alexander Boyd, farmer in Roddingdykes in sheriffdom of Ayr, his spouse, married at New Church of Edinburgh, 16 June 1684. No warrants   .   .   .   I 136   28 June 1694

69. **Process of Adherence**—Mr. Patrick Reid, preacher of the Gospel, against Elizabeth Ogilvie, relict of Mr. James Morison, late minister [of Evie] in Orkney, his spouse, married at Edinburgh in February 1687. Defender assoilzied. No warrants   I 248   19 Aug. 1696

70. **Process of Divorce**—George Prestoune, chirurgeon in Edinburgh, against Mary Boghurst, lawful daughter of William Boghurst, apothecary in London, his spouse, married May 1687 at St. Mary Magdalene's Church, London, Mr. Charles Campbell, co-respondent   I 261   20 Aug. 1696

71. **Process of Divorce on Impotency**—Isobel Macintosh, lawful daughter to William Macintosh in Corryburgh, parish of Moy and sheriffdom of Inverness, against Angus M'Bean, soldier in Colonel Hills regiment, Inverlochy, married at Moy 1687   I 239   7 March 1696

72. **Process of Adherence**—Margaret Seatoune, lawful daughter to the deceased James Seatoun, skipper in Leith, against Edward Callender, youngest son of Edward Callender, merchant, London, her spouse, married October 1693   I 268   9 Sept. 1696

73. **Process of Divorce**—John Grant of Ballindalloch, against Anna Leslie, lawful daughter to [Patrick] Leslie of Balquhoyn, *alias* Count Leslie, his spouse, married 11 November 1682 at Mansion House of Balquhoyn. Captain Charles Gordon in Kirdells, captain in Colonel Lauder's Regiment in Flanders, co-respondent   1696

74. **Process of Adherence**—George, Duke of Gordon, against Elizabeth, now Duchess of Gordon, formerly designed Lady Elizabeth Howard, daughter to the Earl of Norwich, Lord High Marshall of England, thereafter Duke of Norfolk   1696

75. **Process of Scandal**—David Aitchison, deacon of the baxters of Haddington, against James Douglas, baxter, burgess of

A more detailed study of divorce in Scotland is Leah Leneman's *Alienated Affections. The Scottish Experience of Divorce and Separation, 1684-1830,* [Edinburgh University Press, Edinburgh, 1998]. Among the cases dealt with in the book is an early elopement case dating from 1726 when Alexander Herbertson, a wright and looking-glass maker in Glasgow, left his wife, Marion Stewart, and fled to Ireland with Jean Brodie, a servant [NAS.CC8.5.3].

Records of the High Court of the Justiciary

The High Court of the Justiciary of Scotland is the highest criminal court in the land. It dates from the twelfth century but was restructured in 1672. While the court was centred in Edinburgh, provision was also made for circuit courts, the Northern circuit (with courts in Perth, Aberdeen, and Inverness), the Southern circuit (with courts in Dumfries and Jedburgh), and the Western circuit (with courts in Stirling, Glasgow and Ayr). Also until 1746 there was a hereditary justiciarship of Argyll and the Isles. While practically all of the Records of the High Court of Justiciary are in their original manuscript form, now in the National Archives of Scotland, those of Argyll and the Isles have been published: *Justiciary Record of Argyll and the Isles, 1664-1705*, by John Cameron [Stair Society, Edinburgh, 1949] and *The Justiciary Record of Argyll and the Isles, Volume II, 1705-1742*, by John Imrie [Stair Society, Edinburgh, 1969].

These represent an important source for those interested in Highland history but contain only a handful of cases with an Irish connection, including the following:

14 May 1673, John Crawford and Mary NcLauchlane were accused of 'notar adultrie..... contrair to the law of God and the laws and acts of parliament of this kingdome'. In 1664 and 1665 Mary NcLauchlane, being married to Patrick McVicar in Feorling, behaved in the most unchristianly and undutiful way, mixing with lewd and evil company. In 1664 or 1665 she committed adultery, first with Donald, son of Reverend Archibald McCallum minister of

Kilmichael Glassary, whereby there was a child born called More NcCallum, then in 1669 she and the said John Crawford also committed adultery and went to Ireland where they lived for eighteen months, before returning to Knapdale where they cohabited and had two children.

26 August 1680, Andrew Gardner in Drummore was accused of the murder of Duncan McLelland sometime in Ireland about sixteen years previously.

28 August 1680 – Finvall NcCannill in Knockhanti was accused of murdering her own child in 1676, born though her adultery with Malcolm McComy now in Ireland.

Records of the High Court of the Admiralty of Scotland

The Admiralty Court had jurisdiction on all maritime and seafaring cases, both civil and criminal, until 1830 when its civil jurisdiction was transferred to the Court of Session. Up to recently, these records were virtually unusable to all but the most enthusiastic of researchers. The only official guide to this massive documentary collection lies in roughly chronological lists of court cases, which only provide the names of the pursuer, the defender, and a date, with no clue to the case contents. This difficulty has now been overcome, at least for most of the seventeenth century and the first half of the eighteenth century, with the release in 2005 of the CD compiled by the Scottish maritime historians Sue Mowat and Eric J. Graham entitled *High Court of the Admiralty of Scotland, Record 1627-1750,* which provides abstracts for all the cases heard during the period. This source covers the following:

Decreets 1627-1692
Processes 1703-1750
Decrees in absence 1701-1750
Summary warrants 1703 – 1750

Commissions 1693 – 1750
Bonds 1703 – 1750
Criminal Cases 1705 – 1735
Appendices:
The Lord High Admirals of Scotland 1402 – 1707
The Scottish Admirals and Their Courts
The Scottish Contribution to International Maritime Law
Sources of 17th and 18th century Scottish Maritime History

Inevitably, some of the cases have connections with Ireland. In 1715 and 1716 there are a number of interrelated court cases all concerned with the Martin of Dublin, a 60-ton square-sterned vessel [NAS.AC8.185 Ramsay and Auchterlony versus Johnston; NAS.AC9.558, Shannan v. Johnston; Varreilles v. Johnston, 1716; Galt v. Taylor, [NAS.AC9.558 and AC9.581/1 + AC581/2]. Patrick Johnston, once a merchant in Dublin but by 1715 a refugee in Holyrood Abbey, Edinburgh, was sued by George Shannan, carpenter of the Ringsell of Dublin, and by 1716 a shipbuilder in Dublin for the cost of building the said vessel in 1712. Johnston, however, had sold the ship to George Auchterlony, a shipmaster, and Charles Ramsay a merchant in Montrose; but subsequently the court had arrested the ship as security for various debts due by Johnston to his creditors. It is possible that the above Patrick Johnston was the merchant of Edinburgh mentioned in the case of Prince versus Morison on 6 April 1688 [NAS.AC7.9].

Another case, McCulloch versus Allan in 1726 [NAS.AC9.967], is concerned with Captain James McCulloch and company in Belfast, owners of the galley Mary, Captain James Baillie, which was chartered by Robert Allan in Belfast for a voyage to Barbados. However the ship remained in Barbados for six months longer than originally estimated, and McCulloch sued Allan for losses sustained. The case was held in Scotland as the ship was in Glasgow. Among the people named in the court proceedings were James Mears, a merchant in Belfast, and several members of the crew.

Barony Courts

During the medieval period the king allocated grants of lands wherein the local barons were responsible for law and order. Stewartries and bailiaries were royal lands where a steward or bailie ruled on behalf of the king. These, too, had local courts to administer. In the mid-eighteenth century, legislation was introduced transferring the judicial rights of the regality, stewartry and bailiary courts into the hands of the local sheriff, while the powers of the barony courts were significantly reduced.

Some of the records of these courts are now in the National Archives of Scotland in Edinburgh. Among those of south-west Scotland are the following:

Alloway, barony court books for 1581-1607, and from 1611-1617 [NAS.B6.28.2-4].

Busbie, barony court book for 1640-1709, and 1732-1748 [NAS.GD455.29-30].

Carrick, bailiary scroll record, 1663-1718 [NAS.RH11.14.2].

Corshill, barony court book, 1666-1719 [NAS.GD1.300.1].

Cunningham, bailiary court book, 1633-1650, 1660-1701 [NAS.RH11.19.1-5].

Eskdale, regality court rolls, 1695-1748. [NAS.GD224.293]
Court book, 1731-1747 [NAS.SC15.73.1].

Glasgow, regality court book, 1605-1742 [NAS.RH11.32.3-13].

Glenluce, barony court minute book, 1601-1642 [NAS.RH11.33.2].

Kilmarnock, regality court book, 1693-1740 [NAS.RH11.44.1].

Kilwinning, regality court book, 1662-1726 [NAS.RH11.45.1-3].

Kirkcudbright, stewartry court records, 1693-1696 [NAS.DI70.5].

Murraythwaite, baron court minutes, 1704-1714 [NAS.GD219.201].

Paisley, barony court book, 1688-1692, 1697-1705 [NAS.RH11.57.1-2].

Tarbolton, regality proceedings 1705 [NAS.GD220.6.494].

Wamphrey barony court minutes, 1596, 1684, 1687, 1688 [NAS.RH11.69.1; GD111.1.36].

Among the few published transcriptions of such records are the following:

Records of the Baron Court of Stichill, 1655-1807, [Scottish Record Society, Edinburgh, 1905].

Melrose Regality Record, 1547-1706, [Scottish Record Society, Edinburgh, 1914-1917].

Registers of Hornings

When a court made an order or decree against a debtor, the creditor would obtain 'letters of horning,' which ordered the debtor to fulfil his obligation within a fixed period of time. If the debtor failed to pay up within the allotted period, he was denounced as a rebel with three blasts of the horn. For example, George Maxwell of Glenarm failed to honor his bill of exchange made out in favour of Thomas McGeorge in Little Culloch, Kirkcudbrightshire, and was subsequently "put to the horn" by the Sheriff of Kirkcudbright on 11 October 1737. [NAS.D1.70.10/364] Letters of Inhibition would be issued to prevent a debtor selling heritable estate to avoid any claims by a debtor. These records are in the NAS under the reference "DI." Registers of Hornings and Inhibitions exist for most sheriffdoms and some bailieries, regalities and stewartries of the seventeenth and eighteenth centuries:

Ayr, a sheriffdom, for 1590, 1653-1658, and from 1661 onwards [NAS.DI.25/28].

Carrick, a bailiary, from 1697-1748 [NAS.DI.111].

Cunningham, a bailiary, from 1635-1640, 1675-1685, 1693-1709 [NAS.DI.113/114].

Douglas, a regality, for 1710, and from 1718-1738 [NAS.SC38.76.6-7].

Dumfries, a sheriffdom, for 1656-1658, and from 1673 onwards [NAS.DI.44/45].

Dunbarton, a sheriffdom, for 1661-1680, and from 1718 onwards [NAS.DI.42].

Glasgow, a regality, from 1614-1748 [NAS.DI.117/118].

Hamilton, a regality, from 1710-1747 [NAS.DI.119].

Kilwinning, a regality, from 1620-1664, 1675-1703 [NAS.DI.121; RH11.45.2/7].

Kirkcudbright, a sheriffdom, from 1614 onwards [NAS.DI.70/71].

Lanark, a sheriffdom, from 1676 onwards [NAS.DI.72/75/80].

Renfrew, a sheriffdom, from 1661-1676, 1705-1729, and from 1733 onwards [NAS.DI.94/96].

Wigtown, a sheriffdom, from 1620-1630, 1662-1690, 1696-1719, and from 1727 onwards [NAS.DI.108/109].

CHAPTER FOUR
Miscellaneous Government Records

Retours and Services of Heirs

The legal process known as the Services of Heirs—formerly known as Retours, an abbreviation of a Latin phrase, *Inquisitionum Retornatarum Abbreviatio*—record the transfer of inheritance of landed property in Scotland. These can be found among the Chancery Record in the NAS; however, there are excellent published indexes available in major libraries in Scotland.

For the period dating before 1700, there are Latin documents for which there are published abstracts and indexes organised on a county basis from 1545. These abstracts can be found in a rare three volume set of books published in 1811, entitled:

Inquisitiones Specialis, in Inquisitionum ad Capellam Domini Regis Retornatarum quae in Publicis Archivis Scotiae adhuc servantur, abbreviation.

Source: Inquisitiones Specialis, (Dumfries), in Inquisitionum ad Capellam Domini Regis Retornatarum quae in Publicis Archivis Scotiae adhuc servantur, abbreviation, Volume 1, [Edinburgh, 1811].

27 November 1679. Gulielmus Johnstoun, haeres Joannis Johnstone, mercatoris in Carrickfergus in Hibernia, patris, - in 20 mercatis terrarium antique extentus de Benga vocatis Netherfield de Benga, in parochial de Drysdaill et senescallatu de Annandaill.

Which translated from Latin reads as

"William Johnston, heir to John Johnston, a merchant in Carrickfergus, Ireland, his father in 20 merks land of the old extent of Benga known as Netherfield of Benga, in the parish of Drysdale and the Stewartry of Annandale."

Similarly from the same source:

Inquisitiones Specialis, (Kirkcudbright), in Inquisitionum ad Capellam Domini Regis Retornatarum quae in Publicis Archivis Scotiae adhuc servantur, abbreviation, Volume 1, 1811.

24 May 1670 Jacobus Murray in Inshkeill in regno Hibernia, haeres Alexandri Murray de Blalkcraig, patris, - in 3 mercatis terrarium de Blackcraig antique extentus, infra parochiam de Borg, et mercata terrae et tertia parte mercatae terrae de Barcly antique extentus, infra parochiam de Rerrick.

Which in English is:

"James Murray in Inchkeill, in the Kingdom of Ireland, heir to his father Alexander Murray of Blackcraig in 3 merks of land of Blackcraig of the old extent in the parish of Borg, and a merk and a third of land of Barcly in the parish of Rerrick."

From 1700 onward there are the published **Decennial Indexes to the Services of Heirs in Scotland**, in four volumes in English covering the period 1 January 1700 to 31 December 1859. Volume 1 covers the period 1700 to 1749 and was published in Edinburgh in 1863.

One of the earliest of those dating from the eighteenth century was that of John Thomson, a merchant in Colrain to his father John Thomson of Sevenacre, heir general, 18 October 1705, recorded 14.3.1707, monthly number 12.

The original document is recorded In Latin in Volume 52 of the Inquisitionum Retornatarum Registrum held in the National Archives of Scotland [NAS.C22/52/folios 406-407]. Basically the record states that an inquest was held in Irvine, Ayrshire, on 14 March 1707 by James Blair of Certoun, baillie substitute of the Bailliary of Cunningham, together with James Boyle of Montgomeriestoun, Thomas Cunningham of Montgreenan, Richard Cunningham of Bedland, George Fullarton of Dreghorn, Master William Cunningham former provost of Irvine, Adam Fullarton of Bartanholme, James Nisbet former baillie of Irvine, Patrick Boyle of Smiddieshaw, William Barclay of Warrick, John Marshall of Greenhead, Mr John Cumming MD, Hugh Montgomery of Broomlands, William Stevenson a baillie of Irvine, John Blair of Burrowland, and Robert Hastie a merchant in Irvine, who declared that John Thomson a merchant in Coleraine was the son and heir of his father John Thomson of Sevinaferr.

In 1999 the Scottish Genealogy Society published two cd-roms containing the afore mentioned Retours of the Services of Heirs, 1544-1699, and also The Decennial Indexes to the Services of Heirs in Scotland, 1700-1859.

The Register of the Great Seal of Scotland, alias Registrum Magni Sigilli Regnum Scotorum
[re-published in Edinburgh, 1984]

This source records the granting of land by the Sovereign and the confirmation of any subsequent transfer of ownership. The Register of the Great Seal has been published in eleven volumes for the period 1314 to 1668. The original registers, all in Latin manuscript, must be consulted for the period 1669 to 1919. There are, however, indexes in the National Archives of Scotland which facilitate research. All volumes, with the exception of volumes X and XI, are in Latin and are well indexed by surname and title of property concerned. Entries with links to Ireland are extremely rare and are difficult to locate. One of the few in this category is charter 502 in Volume X which covers the period of the Commonwealth between 1652 and 1659:

"Edinburgh, February 8, 1656. The Protector, [that is, Oliver Cromwell], grants to Agnes Maxwall, daughter of the deceased Robert Maxwall, younger, maltman, indweller in the County of Tyrone in Ireland, her heirs and assignees whomsoever, - a laigh dwelling house or ground house, comprehending a hall, foirbuith, chalmer and brewhouse, part of a great tenement of land which pertained of

*old to John Baba, lying within the burgh of Glasgow, on the ......
side of the Hie Street thereof, a little above the Cross, with the
pertinents thereof; - which pertained to the deceased Daniell
Maxwall, merchant burgess of Glasgow, called the Chapman, and
now to the Protector by reason of bastardy, as ultimus haeres, the
said Daniell being born a bastard and so deceasing without lawful
heirs of his body: - to be held of the Protector in free burgage, for
the rights and services used and wont."*

Register of the Privy Council of Scotland
[published in Edinburgh, from 1877 onwards]

Before 1707 this was the main record of Scottish government
and covers a wide range of topics and mentions people at all levels
of society. The Register covers the period from 1545 to 1691 with
the first volume being published in Edinburgh in 1877. The Privy
Council of Scotland ended with the Union of Scotland and England
in 1707, and the register in its manuscript form for the period 1692
to 1707 can be consulted in the National Archives of Scotland. It
contains a considerable number of entries pertaining to Ireland. The
many volumes of the series all are well indexed. The first evidence
of Scottish involvement in the Plantation of Ulster comes in a letter:

*On 19 March 1609 Alexander Hay, the Scottish Secretary of
State in London, wrote to the Privy Council of Scotland announcing
the proposed Plantation of Ulster and encouraged his countrymen
not to miss this great opportunity [RPCS.VII.792-794].*

In the summer of 1609 the Privy Council of Scotland began to
receive applications for lands in Ulster, and by mid September of
that year 77 people had registered their interest in acquiring land
grants varying between 2000 and 1000 acres. They largely came
from the ranks of the lairds, burgesses, and minor branches of the
nobility. Pages lxxxviii-xci of volume VIII of the Register of the Privy
Council of Scotland, 1607-1610 [Edinburgh, 1887] identifies these applicants, the acreage sought, and their cautioners or guarantors. In total,

141,000 acres were applied for, and as a condition of allocation the undertakers were required to settle 48 able bodied adult males on each 2000 acres. In total 3,384 men plus their wives and children would have been required.

The initial list containing data on seventy-seven applicants includes the following:

ADAMSON, JAMES, brother of Mr William Adamson of Graycrook (Craigcrook): surety, Andrew Heriot of Ravelston:- 2000 acres.

AITCHISON, HARRY, in Edinburgh: surety, Mr James Cunningham of Mountgrennan:- 2000 acres.

ALEXANDER, ROBERT, son of Christopher Alexander, burgess of Stirling, surety, his said father:- 1000 acres.

ANDERSON, JAMES, portioner of Little Govan: surety, John Allison in Carsbrig:- 1000 acres.

Not everyone went to Ireland willingly; for example, Lance Armstrong, a thief, was banished to Ireland 1620 [RPCS.XII.288].

The Privy Council also received petitions from Irish residents; for example, on 4 June 1691 it considered one from Louis Thomson, a merchant in Belfast, and George McCartney, late sovereign (mayor) of the town, whose ships had been impressed by the forces of King James to take horses and men from Carrickfergus, Ireland, to Mull, Scotland, in July 1689 [RPCS.XVI.309].

Later that same year, on 15 December, the Privy Council received a petition from Reverend Patrick Dunlop who had fled from Ireland in 1689 and settled in the parish of Minigaff as a minister [RPCS.XVI.609].

Throughout the seventeenth century the Register contains much reference material to Scottish links with Ireland and Ulster in particular. Copies of the Registers can be found in major libraries throughout Scotland, as well as in the National Archives of Scotland and the National Library of Scotland.

In 1683 the Privy Council, wishing to identify the Covenanters and sympathisers in various counties, imposed the Test Oath on all adults there. The test oath basically required them to agree that in no circumstances a subject was justified in taking up arms against his or her sovereign. The oath therefore was designed to identify the militant Presbyterians or Covenanters who were resisting attempts by the Stuart kings to impose Episcopalianism. Resistance to the royal religious policy was particularly strong in the south-west of Scotland in counties such as Lanarkshire, Dumfries-shire, Annandale, and Kirkcudbrightshire. The lists of the inhabitants of these areas have been published in volume VIII, 3rd series, of the RPCS, as can be seen from the following extracts some people chose to flee to Ireland rather than remain and face punishment.

	652	REGISTER OF THE COUNCIL.	1683.

Parish of Avondale.

" AVENDALE PAROCH. William Hamilton of Overtoun, refuses both; James Young of Netherfeild, refuses; M' James Young of Linbank, bandit, no heritor (last two words deleted) ; Thomas Allan of Cauldstream, refuses (delete) b.; M' William Hamilton, portioner ther, ab. living in Edinburgh; William Hairshaw in Udstounheid, refuses; Alexander Murray ther, refuses (delete) b.; John Mershell ther, refuses; John Steill ther, refuses; William Steill ther, refuses; John Gilkreist ther, b.t.; John Hamilton of Collinghill, refuses; Gawin Semple in Overtoun, refuses; William Wilsone in Netherfeild, ab. no heritor nor liferenter; John Alstoun, portioner ther, refuses; John Allan in Netherfeildyke, b.t.; the heretor of Craig, forfault; the heretor of Windhill, forfault; John Steill of Castellbrokit, b. no heritor (last three words delete) ; John Peacok of Chappell, b.t.; John Cochrane ther, ab. fugitive; John Cochrane of Struther, b.t.; John Stuart of Langkyp, b.; John Hamilton of Raws, b.t.; John Bannatyne of Craigmuir, refuses; Allan Jackson in Langkyp, ab.; John Watsone ther, ab.; John Hamilton of Kyp, refuses; Andrew Dyks of St Brydschappell, ab.; William Nimo in Hislybank, b.t.; John Nimo ther, ab.; William Semple ther, refuses; Mungo Dyks of Kirkwood, fugitive; Gawin Semple ther, refuses; William Dyks of Lambhill, refuses; John Semple of Ruchtrie, ab. no heritor; Alexander Small\of Dyks, refuses; James Morisone ther, refuses; James Mairteinholme ther, refuses; John Young of Water, ab.; Mathew Cochrane of Syd, b.t.; John Young ther, ab. named imediatlie befor except on; Thomas Brounlie of Torfoot, fugitive; Thomas Hamilton ther, refuses; John Cuninghame of Enterkin, ab. living out of the shyre; Andrew Hamilton in Litle Drumclog, ab.; Robert Young in Goodsburn, refuses; Andrew

Liper ther, ab. no heritor; John Cochrane of Oversyd, refuses; William
Fleming of Ryding, refuses (last word delete) b.; William Brouning
of Cauldcoats, ab.; John Tailzeor in Syd, refuses (last word delete) b.;
James Cochrane of Bonanhill, refuses; James Hamilton of Struther,
ab. no such man; Robert Dalzell of Rylandsyds airs, ab. minors; John
Dyks of Rylland, refuses (last word delete) b.; James Dyks of
Halburn, forfault; William Cochrane of Brounsyd, refuses; Frances
Carnduf of Caldermiln, b.t.; Thomas Leiper of Feildheid, refuses;
Andro Steill ther, ab. said to be noe heritor; John Steill of Bracanrig,
refuses; John Steill, his sone, refuses; John Rob ther, ab. sick; Claud
Hamilton of Letham, refuses (last word delete) b.; Allan Dukes ther,
refuses (last word delete) b.;   Gilkreist airs ther, minors;
          Allasone airs in Windiedge, ab. living in Ireland; William
Semple of Heuk, refuses; William Steill in Hall of Carnduf, refuses,
therefter signd the band; John Cochrane in Carnduf, refuses (last word
delete) b.; William Allason in Gallowmuirheid, refuses; John Holms
in Newtoun, refuses; John Hart, portioner ther, quaker; William
Fleming in Newtoun, John Fleming in Greathill, ab. no heritor;
William Gilmore in Pristgill, refuses; Robert Gilmore ther, refuses;
James Cochrane ther, refuses; John Aitoun in Heukheid, in prisone;
Robert Allasone of Caldercruiks, b.t.;   Auchinleck of Litle
Hairschaw, ab. woman; William Cochrane of West Newtoun, ab. sick;
James Young of Peillhill, refuses (last word delete) b.; Thomas
Robison in Hisildaine, refuses; Thomas Scot ther, b.t.; Gawin
Hamilton of Castelbrokit, ab. living in Edinburgh, said to be but
adjudger and the heretor hes taken the b.; George Ross of Galston, ab.
living in Ireland; Archbald Stirling of Hilheid, ab. said to be noe
heritor.

"TOUN OF STRATHAVEN. John Frams airs, ab. in Ireland; Town of Strathaven.
Alexander Craig, fugitive; Cudbert Dicks airs, minors; John Mershell,
ab. no heritor; John Stuart, refuses (last word delete) b.; James
Currie, refuses (last word delete) b.; John Hairschaw, ab. in Ireland;
John Hamilton, dead without airs; William Allan, ab.; Robert
Gilkrists airs, ab. in Ireland;   Craigs airs, abs. women;
Alexander Hamilton, refuses (last word delete) b.; Richard Meikle,
ab.;   Smiths airs, minors; William Meikles airs, ab. women;
Marion Hamilton, abs.; Mathew Broun, ab.; John Scott, refuses;
Margaret Willok; John Hamilton, refuses (last word delete) b.; James
Robisone, bandit; Andrew Wilsone, ab.; John Brounlie, b.t.; Grissall
Thomson, relict of Andrew Wilson, abs.; John Carnduf, fugitive;
Margaret Jack, relict of Ja. Meikle, abs.; John Lausone, ab.; Androw
Broun, refuses; Mathew Cochrane, ab.; John Law, ab.; Alexander
Morton, b.t.; James Tennent, v.; Helen Riddell, ab.; John Archbald,
b.t.; Thomas Hamilton, living in Carrik; Gawin Murrays airs, ab. a
woman; Helen Robisone, dead and hir airs minor; James Auchinleck,
ab. no heritor; Andro Davidson, living in Louthian; Gawin Or,
refuses; Simon Andersone, b.; Mathew Loudoun, ab.; Walter
Evinsone, b.t.; James Lausons airs, ab. in Ireland; Michaell
Mershell, refuses; John Hamiltons airs, minors; Mungo Cochrane,
ab.; Andro Tennant, refuses (last word delete) b.; William Gebbie,
refuses, refuses (last two words delete) b.; John Loudoun, b.t.; Andro
Hamiltons airs; John Dick, refuses (last word delete) b.; John
Sliman, ab.; John Ramage, ab.; Robert Leiper, refuses (last word
delete) b.; Thomas Brounlie, ab.; Hew Purveance, refuses (last word
delete) b.; George Arcle, ab.; William Cochrans, sick and up befor;
Patrick Lochore, b.; John Cochrane, refuses (last word delete) b.;
James Muirs airs, ab. no representatives;   Steills airs, minors;
Walter Hamilton, b.t.; John Auld, b.t.

Port books

These exist to varying degrees for most of the ports of Scotland during the seventeenth century. After the Union of Parliaments of Scotland and England in 1707, the practice of maintaining a record of cargoes in and out, the ships, shipmasters and merchants involved was discontinued until 1742. From that date until the 1820s, there are virtually comprehensive records of shipping and cargoes in and out of Scottish ports, the NAS.E504 series. The port-books of the seventeenth century can be consulted in the NAS; there are two series: the first [E71 series] covering the period 1478 to 1640 and the second 1660s-1690s [E72 series]. A few of such records also exist among the Laing manuscripts in Edinburgh University Library [reference Laing MSS.La.II.490-491].

The ports which contain the vast majority of references to Ireland were, naturally, those in south-west Scotland from Glasgow on the River Clyde to the Solway Firth. Customs precincts were established which contained a main port and a number of subsidiary ports; for example, Irvine included Largs, Portincross and Saltcoats.

The Customs collectors' function was to record the taxable imports and exports and they had little interest in passengers unless they were carrying goods. Occasionally there are entries such as James Hamilton, a passenger on the <u>Katherine of Larne</u> which arrived in Ayr on 20 August 1673. [NAS.E72.3.3] However, the names of the shipmasters are given as are the port of registration of their vessels. As the skippers are highly likely to be resident in these ports, this reveals where a particular family is known to reside at that time.

Port books of south-west Scotland dating before 1707

Ayr. These date from 1559 [NAS.E71/3; E72/3; E74; E78/6].

Dumbarton. These date from 1613 [NAS.E71/9; E74].

Dumfries. These date from 1577 [NAS.E71/10; E72/6; E74].

Glasgow. These date from 1665 [NAS.E72/10; E78/6].

Irvine. These date from 1561 [NAS.E71/19; E72/12; E74; E78/6].

Kirkcudbright. These date from 1639 [NAS.E73/9; E74].

Port Glasgow. These date from 1680 [NAS.E72/19; E74].

Portpatrick. These date from 1671 [NAS.E72/20; E74].

Port books of south-west Scotland dating after 1742
The Customs Collectors Quarterly Accounts

Ayr. 1742 to 1748, 1748 to 1756 [NAS.E504.4.1/2].

Dumfries. 1743 to 1748, 1748 to 1756 [NAS.E504.9.1/2].

Greenock. 1742 to 1744, 1744 to 1746, 1746 to 1748, 1748 to 1750 [NAS.E504.1/2/3/4].

Irvine. 1742 to 1748, 1748 to 1752 [NAS.E504.18.1/2].

Kirkcudbright. 1742 to 1748, 1748 to 1752 [NAS.E504.21.1/2].

Port Glasgow. 1742 to 1744, 1744 to 1746, 1746 to 1748, 1748 to 1750 [NAS.E504.28.1/2/3/4].

Port Patrick. 1742-1748, 1748 to 1750 [NAS.E504.29.1/2].

Stranraer. 1742 to 1748, 1748 to 1756 [NAS.E504.34.1/2].

Wigtown. 1742 to 1748, 1748 to 1766 [NAS.E504.37.1/2].

Property

During the sixteenth century and up to 1617, notaries maintained 'protocol books' which record the transfer of land ownership. Abstracts from some of those pertaining to Ayr have been published in **Archaeological and Historical Collections relating to Ayrshire and Galloway**, Volume VI, (Ayr Archaeological and Natural History Society, Edinburgh, 1889). The Protocol Books for twenty-eight burghs are extant and include Ayr from 1586, Dumfries from 1585, Irvine from 1611, and Kirkcudbright from 1625. Most of these are in the appropriate local archives; for example, Glasgow Archives has the Burgh Protocol Book from 1547.

The Glasgow protocols have been published in eleven volumes for the period 1547 to 1600 in a series published in Glasgow between 1894 and 1900 entitled **Abstracts of Protocols of the Town Clerks of Glasgow**. The first volume represents the protocol book of William Hegait from 1547 to 1555, while volume eleven covers the period 1591 to 1600 and the protocols of the notaries George Huchesone and Henry Gibsone. These books are highly indexed both on a personal and locational basis.

The last of the entries is dated *"29 December 1600 at 2 pm. John Stark, junior, merchant, citizen, for the love he bore towards John Stark, son of him and Agnes Pollock, spouses, and at the request of Charles Pollock, father of Agnes, resigned in favour of his son a back tenement, under and above, with the pertinents, lying, in the territory and the city of Glasgow, on the west side of the street leading from the market cross to the South Nether Port, between the lands of William Flemyng on the east, of Archibald Miller on the west, and of William Coningham on the north, and of Mark Knox on the south; but reserving the liferent of Charles Pollock, and after his decease the liferents of John Stark, senior, and Agnes Pollok. Sasine given by Robert Rowat, bailie. Witnesses: Mark Knox, merchant, Andrew Scherar, cooper, Finlay Allasoun, weaver, citizens, Robert Herbertsoun, notary, Stephen Seller and John Pawtone, officers."*

In 1599 it was enacted that there should be a register of sasines and related writs. Subsequently, the country was divided into 17 districts. Some of these records survive for the period up to 1609 and are known as the Secretary's Register. For example, there are four volumes for the period 1599 to 1609 entitled **The Secretary's Registers for Ayr and the Bailiaries of Kyle, Carrick and Cunninghame** [NAS.RS11-14], for which there is an index to persons.

From 1617 until recently, it was necessary to record writs in either the General Register of Sasines in Edinburgh or with the Particular Registers of the counties. This did not apply to sasines within the royal burghs which maintained their own registers. There are, for example, **Particular Registers of Sasines for Dumfries and the Stewartries of Kirkcudbright and Annandale** covering the periods 1617 to 1660 and from 1671 to 1869 [NAS.RS22-RS23] which comprise 205 volumes. There are published indexes to persons 1617 to 1780 and to persons and places 1675 to 1722 in NAS.RS23/2-9; also persons and places 1671 to 1793 in NAS.RS87/1-11.

There are also published indexes for Argyll, Dumbarton, Bute, Arran and Tarbet, 1617-1780 [NAS.RS9-10] and Lanark, 1618-1780 [NAS.RS40-42]. As yet, there is no published index to Wigtown [NAS.RS60-61].

Source: Particular Register of Sasines for Ayrshire, Secretary's Register, Volume V.

1 November 1632, registration of renunciation by Jonet Campbell, eldest lawful daughter of the deceased Mr Alexander Campbell, minister of the gospel at Stevenstoun, narrating her marriage with John Peibles, younger of Pethirland, indweller in the parish of Balliemony in County Antrim, Ireland, which took place in Ireland, and that the said John Peibles had lately obtained a decree of divorce against her before Mr John Monypennie, Doctor of Divinity, principal officer and general commissary to Robert, Bishop of Down and Conver, because that she in the year 1621 been contracted in marriage and bethrothed to the deceased James Bryding in presence of several witnesses, whereby she was found to have been married to him and so her marriage with John Peibles was found of nullity, which sentence of divorce was read and published in the parish kirk of Ballimonie on 6 October last in presence of Thomas Tayleour, notary, registrar of Troyist, and other witnesses; and now because the said John Peibles has repaid to her all the sums of money and others which were given by her and the deceased Elizabeth Smeittoun, her mother, and Thomas Boyd of Carncogie, her spouse, or others her friends in name of tocher with her, she discharges him thereof and renounces the liferent infeftment which received from him of the half of his lands of Pethirland in the parish of Beyth and bailiary of Cunningham, and also the joint fee of his lands of Tulloger held by the said John Peiblis of the Earl of Antrim in the parish of Balliemonie, with all right to an annuity of £5.11 shillings sterling, which John Peiblis of Peddirland, father of the said John, is obliged to pay to her after the said John's decease in terms of a decreet arbitral between the said John Peiblis, younger, and the said Thomas Boyd of Carncogie, dated 20 December 1626. The Renunciation is dated at Irvine 13 November 1632; witnesses Allan Dunlope, provost of Irvine, William Cauldwell of Annanhill, baillie clerk of Cunningham, Christiern Cunningham, uncle to the Laird of Robertland, Mr William Russell, minister at Kilbirney, Robert Broun, town clerk of Irvine, and Mathew Homill, his servitor.

Source: as above, Volume VII.

15 November 1642. Registration of Renunciation by Hew Thomsoun, sometime in Rebegge in County Antrim, and now in Halls of Bargoure, in favour of John, Earl of Loudoun, of the £3.3.4, lands of Bargoure, which were wadset by the said Earl, then Lord Loudoun, to him on 31 December 1639, for 4000 merks and which the said Lord of Loudoun acquired from the deceased George Campbell of Horscleuch, and are now occupied by Andrew Gilchrist, Alexander Gibsoun and James Reid, his tenants, lying in the barony of Kylesmure and bailliary of Kyle Stewart. The redemption money having been paid the lands are hereby renounced at Mauchline, 10 November 1642; witnesses James Thomsoun, eldest lawful son of the renouncer, William Farquhar in Aird, John Campbell, son to George Campbell at Burnside, Charles Dalrymple, son to Mr Andrew Dalrymple, notary in Mauchline, and James Mairshell, notary there.

Among the burgh register of sasines are those of Annan from 1762, Ayr from 1597, Dumfries from 1668, Edinburgh from 1682, Irvine from 1721, Kirkcudbright from 1681, Lanark from 1616, New Galloway from 1760, Sanquhar from 1718, Stranraer from 1683, Whithorn from 1684, and Wigtown from 1724. These can be found partly in national archives and partly in local archives.

Source: Edinburgh City Archives: Moses bundle #176/6941
Janet Simpson, wife of Alexander Seton in Hillsborough, Ireland, the only daughter and heir of William Simpson a gardener in Erskine, subscribed to an Instrument of Sasine on 3 March 1705.

102   **AYR—REGISTER OF SASINES, 1617-1634.**

Name and Designation.	Date of Recording.	Vol.	Fol.	County or Sheriffdom.
CUIK, Gilbert, in Ireland, son of John C., weaver, Maybole (*bis*)	4 July 1619	1	359	Ayr
„ „ „ „ „	4 Apr. 1625	3	306	„
„ James, son of John C. in Lowdounhill	30 July 1627	4	89	„
„ Janet, spouse of John M'Alexander, weaver, Maybole.	4 „ 1619	1	359	„
„ John, in Lowdounhill	31 Aug. 1625	3	394	„
„ „ „	30 July 1627	4	89	„
„ „ „ elder	24 Feb. 1626	3	525	„
„ „ „ younger	24 „ 1626	3	525	„
„ „ weaver, Maybole	4 July 1619	1	359	„
„ „ „ „	4 Apr. 1625	3	306	„
„ „ son of John C. in Lowdounhill	31 Aug. 1625	3	394	„
„ Katherine (? Knok), spouse of John Lymane, weaver, Maybole.	6 „ 1628	4	273	„
„ Marion Couper, relict of John, weaver, Maybole (*bis*)	4 July 1619	1	359	„
CUMMING, Agnes, spouse of Robert Smyth, cooper, Kilmaurs.	8 Jan. 1620	1	403	„
„ „ Or, spouse of Peter, merchant, Kilmaurs.	19 May 1624	3	76	„

Hearth Tax Records, 1691-1695

In 1690 the Scots Parliament ordered that a tax be levied on every hearth within the kingdom at a rate of fourteen shillings per hearth. This tax was imposed to raise funds to pay for the armies opposing the Jacobites. Only hospitals and the very poor were exempt. These survive for much of Scotland; see NAS.E69 series. Only a few have been published. Among them are three from the south west of Scotland, one being H. C. Jones's *The Wigtownshire Hearth Tax Collection* [Scottish Record Society, Edinburgh, 1979]; another covering Dumfries-shire was published as "The Hearth Tax" by D. Adamson in Volumes XLVII and XLIX in the journal *The Transactions of the Dumfries and Galloway Antiquarian Society* [1971-1973]; and the Hearth Tax for Ayrshire, 1691. These records reveal the heads of families who were living within the various parishes in the early 1690s, the number of hearths in each house, and the amount of tax paid. There are also partial lists of the poor of each parish, who were exempt from the tax (see, for example, NAS.GD26.7.357.2). The data for each county is organised by parish and, in the case of rural parishes, by farms or principal landowners holdings within the parish. For example, the parish of Ruthwell in Dumfries-shire contained 154 hearths mostly on the lands of the Viscount of Stormonth, some on the lands of the Earl of Nithsdale, and the rest on the farms of Holmans and of Ramerskeels. Ramerskeels contained four hearths: one of John Coupland at Heugh, one of William Edgar the younger, one by Jean Richardson the younger, and another by John Logan a tailor. The original documents can be consulted in the National Archives of Scotland mostly under the call number NAS.E69 with a few under NAS.GD26.7.300-391.

An extract from the Hearth Tax returns for Dumfries

DUMFREISE PAROCH

Crossquarter

(1) John Grive and M r W a i t t e r (younger, wiver) 1
(2) John W i l s o n turner 1
(3) Jannet Sharp 1
(4) Bailzie Irvin of Logon 7
(5) George Johnstone mert ., ... 3
(6) John Herries 3
(7) Rot Ritchartsone 4
(8) J o h n Johnstone mert 3
(9) Tho and William R i t c h e r t s (Ritchertson) 2
(10) Agnus Glen 2
(11) Dav Bartoun 5
(12) John Japhray 3
(13) Agnus Maxuell ... 1
(14) Margaret B r o u n 1
(15) Gabriell Alisone of Dunjap 3
(16) R o t Johnstone merchant 2
(17) Janet W i l s o n e widow 1

(18) Katarine John- stone widow 1
(19) William Robson chapman 1
(20) 'Mr S a m u e l l Mouitt 1
(21) Thomas Davidsone 1
(22) Katarine Broun ... 4
(23) Thomas Gled- stones 1
(24) Andrew Corsbie 2
(25) Jean Glencorse ... 3
(26) Baillie Irvine of Dumcoutrine ... 3
(27) Andrew Euart ... 1
(28) Adam ' Garnochan (Gunochan) 1
(29) Mrs Muerhead ... 4
(30) James Younge ... 2
(31) Mr Rot Edgar ... 3
(32) Samuell Gordon 3
(33) Mr Drummond ... 2
(34) Dr John Maxuel 2
(35) Edward Patersone 2
(36) Adam Thompsone 2
(37) Rot Uining 1
(38) Thomas Leuers ... 1
(39) Rot Milligane ... 2

(40) John Reid 2
(41) George Beck 2
(42) John Neuell 2
(43) Baillie Kennen ... 2
(44) Mr James Hume 2
(45) Rot M a x u e l l (Munnell) 3
(46) John Welch 3
(47) M r W i l l i a m Mcjor 1
(48) Mr A l e x a n d e r Strang 2
(49) Mr Dumbar 5
(50) John Andersone mert 3
(51) Charles Logon ... 1
(52) Adam Strudgeon 1
(53) William Simpsone 1
(54) Margaret M'Kclaim- rock (M'Clamar- ock) 3
(55) John Munnell ... 1
(56) John Martine elder mert 1
(57) William Maxwell sadler 1
(58) Thomas Rodger- sone 1

The Poll Tax, 1694 to 1703

This was another tax imposed by the Scottish Parliament to raise funds to pay off debts and to pay arrears of pay due to the army. The amount due by each individual was based on rank and means, while the very poor and children were exempt. The surviving records are incomplete but exist in part for areas such as Edinburgh, Ayrshire, Berwickshire, Renfrewshire, Selkirkshire, and Glasgow; see NAS.E70 series. These are virtually censuses of the heads of house-holds for the period and can provide quite specific places of resi-dence. The original manuscripts can be found in the National Ar-chives of Scotland, in Edinburgh City Archives, and other reposito-ries. A few are in print; the most accessible ones are probably Mar-garet Wood's *The Edinburgh Poll Tax Returns for 1694*, which was published by the Scottish Record Society in Edinburgh during 1951, and Frances McDonnell's *The Burgh of Paisley Poll Tax of 1695* [pp, St Andrews, 1995].

Lawson or Dobson, Janet, wife of John Lawson, no stock.

——, Margaret. *See* Wilson.

——, Marion. *See* Gray.

Learmonth, Jean. *See* Pow.

——, Mr Thomas; children, William, Margaret, Anna, Marjorie and Elizabeth; daughter-in-law, Susanna Carse, widow of John Learmonth, doctor of physic; men servants, James Clapperton and George Gordon, unpaid; women servants, Helen Glen, at £27, Margaret Reid and Janet Clerk, each at £17 a year. Ten hearths "in that part of Patrick Steils Land whereof the entrie is in Borthwicks close."

Lee, Martha Lockhart, Lady, whose husband would have paid £24; Barbara Lockhart, wife of James Lockhart of Castlehill, her husband being out of the country; men servants, Mr John Currie, at 100 merks; William Milne and William Taylor, boys and unpaid; women servants, Christian Gillespie, at £48, Margaret Baillie, at £36, Robina Scott, at £16, Margaret Weir, at £24; Elizabeth Shaw, at £20 and bounty, Bessie Whitelaw at £20 and bounty, Isobel Murray, unpaid; lodger, Robina, daughter to Captain John Lockhart.

Legatt or Wilkie, Janet, widow of Robert Legatt, writer; daughter, Isobel.

——, William, procurator; wife; Margaret Ballantyne; children, David, William, Harry, John, Margaret, Marion and Elizabeth, the oldest under 13 years, and Catherine "a sucking child in the Dean and nursing with John Johnstoun meason his wyff ther"; men servants, Anthony Forrester, Ninian Ballantyne, Alexander Home, "who have no fie but what they gain as drink money in the said William, his service"; women servants, Bessie Alison and Anna Murray, each at £12 a year and shoes. Five hearths.

——, Elizabeth, no stock.

Leith, James, writer, servant to Mr John Stewart, advocate, son to Blackhall, in Conn's Close; wife, Anna Cheyne; children, Robert, Louis, about 10 years, at Liberton in Louis Johnston's house, James, about 5 years, also at Liberton in Samuel Ker's house, Anna, about 4 months, at Dalkeith with a nurse; servant, Margaret Christie, at £12 a year. Two hearths.

Lennox, or M'Clelland, Janet, widow of Robert Lennox, glover, "for my worth I do not know"; lodger, Catherine Chambers, widow of John M'Dougall, merchant.

Leslie, Mr George, bookseller, worth under 5,000 merks; wife, Alison Law; her sister, Grizel Law; father-in-law (*sic*), Mr Henry Rymer, minister at Carnbie "who having another settled in his place because of his age stayes with me at present." Five hearths.

——, John, no stock; wife.

Letham, John, elder, indweller, no stock; his wife; servant, Marjorie Striven at £10 a year.

Lidderdale or Pillans, Helen, widow of Mr Robert Lidderdale, regent, no stock; children, James and Mary; servant, Jean Brown, at £12 a year. Three hearths.

Lindsay or Paton, Anna, widow of James Lindsay, wright, worth about £1,000 at his death; daughters, Grizel and Mary.

——, Mr Hercules, outed minister; wife; child, David, under 16 years.

——, John, dyer, worth between 300 and 500 merks; wife, Agnes Hamil-

BURGH OF PAISLEY POLL TAX ROLL
1695

List of the Town

A

ADAM, CATHERINE, spouse of John WHYTE
ADAM, ISOBELL, daughter of John ADAM, wright
ADAM, ISSOBALL, spouse of Robert PARK, maltman
ADAM, JAMES
ADAM, JENNET, daughter of John ADAM
ADAM, JOHN, servant to William Whyte
ADAM, JOHN, son of John ADAM
ADAM, JOHN, late baillie
ADAM, JOHN, household of John Vass
ADAM, JOHN, father of Margaret ADAM, spouse of John Vass
ADAM, JOHN, wright
ADAM, JOHN, son of John ADAM, wright
ADAM, MARGARET, spouse of John VASS
ADAM, MARGARET, household of John VASS
ADAM, MARGARET, spouse of Robert SHEDDEN
ADAM, MARGARET, wife of Patrick CALDWALL, church officer
ADAM, MARGARET, daughter of John ADAM, wright
ADAM, MARGARET, servant in household of James Gardiner
ADAM, MARGARET, widow
ADAM, ROBERT, merchant
ADAM, ROBERT, son of John ADAM, wright
ADAM, THOMAS, son of John ADAM, wright
ADMOUNT, AGNES, servant to Mr Thomas Blackwell, minister
AITKEN, ELIZABETH, widow
AITKEN, ISSOBELL, servant to Matthew Corss, maltman
AITKEN, JOHN, journeyman in Claud Fleming household
AITKEN, ROBERT, yr
ALEXANDER, AGNES, spouse of William KING, weaver
ALEXANDER, CATHERINE, servant in household of William Alexander, late
  baillie

Military Records

The outbreak of the Irish Rebellion in 1641 posed a threat to the Covenanters in Scotland, and their countrymen settled in Ireland. In October 1641 the Scots Parliament met and agreed to have troops ready to send to Ulster if requested by the English government. Subsequently 10,000 troops were despatched to Ireland from Scotland to defend the Protestant communities there. This army established the right of the Scots to protect her Ulster Plantation despite it being within the jurisdiction of England; it also led to the firm establishment of Presbyterianism there. A number of the soldiers married local girls, and some may well have settled there before the army was withdrawn in 1646. Probably the most prominent of the soldiers who married and settled in Ulster was Major General Robert Monro who died on his wife's estate in County Down around 1680. His son Andrew was killed at the siege of Limerick in 1690, while his younger brother Daniel was granted lands in County Down in the 1660s and founded a landed family there.

While there are records of the Scots Army that served in Ulster during the mid-seventeenth century, they are scattered throughout the country. The best single source for researching these collections of military documents can be found in these publications: *A Military Source List, Part One. A Guide to Sources for Military History in private records held by the Scottish Record Office* [SRO, Edinburgh, 1996] and *A Military Source List, Part Two. A Guide to Sources on Military History in government and other records held by the Scottish Record Office* [SRO, Edinburgh, 1996].

To illustrate the kind of document that may be found, notice the following examples:

"November 15, 12 December 1640. Letters on the military situation including mention of Alasdair (MacColla) MacDonald's arrival in Islay from Ireland with seventy men" [NAS.GD112.39.83.4-7; 83.4].

"March 1645, Warrant by the Committee of Moneys for payment of certain sums to Sir William Cochrane of Cowdoun and James McDougall of Garthland for their expenses going to Ireland as therein mentioned, with receipt annexed by Cochrane" [NAS.PA7.3.102].

However, probably the best sources which can be used to identify the Scottish soldiers who served in Ireland during the 1640s are to be found in the National Archives in London. There are two almost complete sets of muster rolls dated 1642 covering the ten regiments of foot and two each of the general's lifeguards of horse and foot. They are mostly referenced NA.SP.28.120, in the Commonwealth Exchequer Papers, with two in the State Papers, Domestic, referenced NA.SP.16.492.58 and NA.SP.16.539.1.105.

CHAPTER FIVE
University Records, Family and Estate Papers, Maps, Plans, and Other Sources

University Records

During the seventeenth and eighteenth centuries, Scotland had five colleges or universities; namely, Glasgow University, Edinburgh University, St Andrews University, Marischal College and King's College [the latter two merged to form the University of Aberdeen in the mid-nineteenth century]. As the sons of the Scottish settlers in Ireland were predominantly Presbyterian, they were automatically excluded from the only contemporary Irish University, Trinity College in Dublin, or the two English universities, Oxford and Cambridge, which were only open to Anglicans. Therefore, anyone from the Scottish communities in Ireland wishing to enter a centre of higher learning almost automatically headed for Scotland and the University of Glasgow in particular but also the University of Edinburgh to a limited extent. The Aberdeen colleges, and St Andrews attracted students from Ireland to a lesser extent, as these centres were associated with Jacobitism and Episcopalianism and thus had little appeal to Ulster Presbyterians. A considerable number of the young men from Ireland who flocked to study in Glasgow became Presbyterian ministers in due course, some in Ireland, the others in Scotland and America. These university-educated young men subsequently formed the elite of the Scotch-Irish communities in Ireland and America. *The Munimenta Alme Universitatis Glasguensis, 1450-1727,* Volume III [Glasgow, 1854], is probably the best source listing students at the University of Glasgow and their nationalities for the period 1593-1727. For the period after 1727, see *A Roll of the Graduates of the University of Glasgow, 1727 to 1897,* W. Innes Anderson, [Glasgow, 1898], and *The Matriculation Albums of the University of Glasgow from 1728 to 1858,*W. Innes Anderson, [Glasgow, 1913].

Extract from *A Roll of the Graduates of the University of Glasgow from 1728 to 1858*:

RODGERS, ANDREW, M.A. 1774.
"Filius natu sextus Jacobi Mercatoris in Comitatu de Cavan et Parochia Kildalan" [Matric. Alb. 1771].

RODGERS, JAMES, C.M. 1823.
"Hibernus" [Grad. Alb.].

RODGERS, JAMES MAXWELL, B.A. 1845, M.A. 1848.
Presbyterian Minister at (1) Kilrea, 1853-69, (2) Londonderry since 1869.

RODGERS, JOHN, M.A. 1821, C.M. 1824.
Brother of Moses Rodgers, M.A. 1821 (q.v.), and "Filius natu Secundus Joannis agricolae in parochia de Drumragh in comitatu de Tyrone" [Matric. Alb. 1818].

RODGERS, JOHN WALKER, B.A. 1845, M.A. 1847.
Inspector of National Schools, (1) Armagh, (2) Belfast.

RODGERS, MAXWELL, M.D. 1857.
Inspector-General, R.N.

RODGERS, MOSES, M.A. 1821.
Intended for Ministry of Irish Presbyterian Church, but never admitted as a Licentiate; emigrated to the United States and died there "sometime in the sixties."

RODGERSON, WILLIAM PATRICK, B.Sc. 1879, M.A. 1880.
U.P. Minister at Lasswade.

RODMAN, ROBERT, M.B., C.M. 1871.
Glasgow; Chascomus, Buenos Ayres; died there, 10th October, 1895.

ROE, EDWARD, M.A. 1774.
"Hibernus" [Grad. Alb.].

ROE, EDWARD THOMAS, M.D. 1841.
Plymouth; Kingskerswell, Devon; London; died 28th September, 1884, aged 64.

ROEBURN, JAMES, M.A. 1779, M.D. 1783.
"Natus in Kirkintilloch Filius natu Maximus Mathae Coactoris tributorum in Comitatu de Dumbarton" [Matric. Alb. 1774].

ROGER, FRANCIS, M.D. 1801.
"Gallus Emigrans" [Grad. Alb.].

ROGERS, DAVID, M.A. 1814.
Possibly the same person as David Rodgers, Irish Presbyterian Minister at Killala, 1820-59, who died June, 1859.

ROGERS, JAMES, M.D. 1833.
Saltash, Cornwall; previously Physician to British Legation, St. Petersburg.

ROGERS, JOHN, M.A. 1764.
Ordained Minister at Ballibay (*alias* Cahans) in 1767, and acted as Professor of Divinity to Irish Burgher Synod from 1796-1814; died 24th August, 1814.

The other published sources on students at Scottish universities during the period are as follows:

Catalogue of Graduates in Faculties of Arts, Divinity and Law of the University of Edinburgh [Edinburgh University Press, Edinburgh, 1858].

List of the Graduates in Medicine in the University of Edinburgh from 1705 to 1865 [Edinburgh University Press, Edinburgh, 1867].

Officers and Graduates of University and King's College, Aberdeen, 1595-1860, P. J. Anderson [Aberdeen University Press, Aberdeen, 1893].

Fasti Academiae Mariscallanae, Aberdonensis, 1593-1890, P. J. Anderson [Aberdeen University Press, Aberdeen, 1898].

Biographical Register of the University of St Andrews, 1747-1897, R. N. Smart [St Andrews, 2004, typescript].

University archives contain substantial collections of historical documents. One of the collections in Edinburgh University library is the **Laing Manuscripts**. Here, too, can be found manuscripts of relevance. For example, there are the 'Rental and Accounts of Sir Claud Hamilton's lands in Ireland' dating from 1613 to 1629, a total of fifty-four pages. The tenants generally seem to be Irish, but there are also a number of Scots:

> *"The towne land of Cullkurrye given be umquhill Sir Claud to Doctor Robert Hamiltoun'* and *'Avischevodan, sett to Gilespie McDonald."*

Family and Estate Papers

Since the medieval period, a significant proportion of Scotland has been in the hands of a relatively small number of land-owning, often aristocratic, families. By necessity they found it essential to maintain records relating to their property as well as personal correspondence.

Some of these families, generally from south western Scotland, acquired land in Ulster during the period of the Plantation, and their records are potentially of significance to those searching for their Scots-Irish roots. Such families on acquiring land in Ireland would recruit tenants and settlers from among their own lands before moving over to Ulster. While some of such estate and family papers remain in private hands, a number have been deposited in archives, such as the National Archives of Scotland where they are available for consultation.

Rentals and tacks (leases) identify tenants, and the property they leased can be found in family of estate papers. There was no legal requirement to preserve the documents once the contract had expired; nevertheless, a number of such Records have survived in a number of archives of landed estates. Take, for example, the Agnews of Lochnaw. This family acquired lands in Wigtownshire from around 1426 and eventually owned land around Lochnaw Castle in the parishes of Leswalt, Kirkcolm, Sorbie, and Inch. In 1636 they acquired a leasehold estate in the parish of Kilwaghter and barony of Glenarm, County Antrim, from the Earl of Antrim. **The Agnew of Lochnaw Muniments** contain papers relating to their Irish estates between 1636 and 1712 and may be accessed in the National Archives of Scotland under reference NAS.GD154.505-534. These do include tacks or leases both for their Scottish and Irish estates. To illustrate this point, there are the leases of his lands in Ireland granted by Andrew Agnew in 1646 to men bearing Scottish names such as Andrew Blair, John Young, Alexander Dunlop, Patrick Agnew, Ninian Montgomerie, Thomas Steill, John Mure, John Blair, William McChachie, and Alexander Dundas. It is likely that the Agnews, in common with the other landowners who were granted lands in Ulster, recruited settlers for Ireland from among their own tenants in Wigtownshire.

Another such collection, also in the National Archives of Scotland, is the **Maxwell of Orchardton papers** [NAS.RH15.91.59], the muniments of a landed family from Kirkcudbrightshire. Among this collection are a number of leases made by Lord Kirkcudbright to tenant farmers, mainly bearing Lowland Scots surnames, in various Londonderry parishes. For example, a lease to Peter Cunningham,

David Murray, and Robert Blair in Dunboe parish, County Londonderry, of the townland of Bellywolerikbeg in the said parish, within the manor of Clothworkers for 11 years, dated 2 July 1655.

Similarly, a branch of the Edmonstone family of Stirlingshire was established in County Antrim during the early seventeenth century and among the **Calendar of Duntreath Muniments** [NAS.GD97] are a number of documents referring to the Edmonestones and their tenants in Ulster. Also the collection includes the marriage contract of Helen, widow of William Adair of Ballymaneoch or Kinhilt, and Archibald Edmonstone of Braidisland dated 17 April 1666 [NAS.GD97.Sec.1.501].

There are a few examples of published family papers of possible relevance such as *The Charter Chest of the Earldom of Wigtown, 1214-1681,* F. J. Grant [Scottish Record Society, Edinburgh, 1910] and *Some Family Papers of the Hunters of Hunterston* [SRS, Edinburgh, 1925].

Unique manuscript collections of potential relevance—such as family and estate papers, burgh and church records—can be found in the following list of archives, libraries and museums in south-west Scotland:

AYRSHIRE ARCHIVES,
Craigie Estate, Ayr. KA8 0SS
Contains:

Kennedy of Kirkmichael papers 1453-1832

Hamilton of Rozelle and Carcluie papers 1734-1926

Kirk Session Record for the Church of Scotland and dissenting Presbyterian congregations within the Presbytery of Ayr, 1615-1983

DUMFRIES ARCHIVES,
33 Burns Street, Dumfries. DG1 2PS
Contains:

Dumfries burgh records from 1506

Dumfriesshire records from 1667

Kirkcudbrightshire records from 1728

Wigtownshire records from 1736

Records of the Seven Trades of Dumfries 1612-1890

Grierson of Lag papers 1518-1761

Stewart of Shambellie papers 1590-1961

McCartney of Halketleaths papers 1560-1830

Maxwell of Munches, of Barncleugh, of Elsieshields, and of Terregles 1450-1898

Copland of Collieston papers 1555-1928

Arnott of Kirkconnel Hall papers 1647-1876

McClellan of Chapeltown and Borness papers 1667-1804

Thomson of Ingleston papers 1646-1824

Clerk Maxwell of Middlebie papers 1640s-1850s

Beattock writs 1703-1859

Culvennan charters 1400s-1800s

Dumfries Kirk Session Records 1648-1960

Troqueer and Maxwelltown Kirk Session Records 1648-1975

Kirkbean Kirk Session Records 1714-1876

Morton, Glencairn and Penpont Kirk Session Records, 1714-1978

Records of Dumfries Presbytery 1647-1885

Abridgements and indexes to the sasines of Dumfries-shire, Kirkcudbright-shire, and Wigtown-shire, 1617-1970.

Dumfries and Galloway Archives also have – Dumfries Kirk Session Records and Presbytery Minutes, 1687-1795;

Mouswald Kirk Session Records 1640-1659

Dumfries Jail Books and Bail Bond Register, 1714-1810;

Troqueer Kirk Session Records, 1698-1771, transcribed!

EAST AYRSHIRE ARCHIVES
Baird Institute, 3 Logar Street, Cumnock. KA18 1AD
Contains:

Kilmarnock burgh records, 1686-1975

GLASGOW CITY ARCHIVES
Mitchell Library, North Street, Glasgow. G37DN
Contains:

Glasgow and neighbouring burgh records, for example -

Records of Rutherglen from 1542

Records of Hutchesons' Hospital, 1579-1958

Campbell of Succoth and Garslube, 1533-1965

Colquhoun of Luss papers, 1188-C20

Hamilton of Barns papers, 1537-1827

Houstoun of Johnstone papers, 1664-1951

Stirling Maxwell of Pollok papers, 1200-1919

Stirling of Keir papers, 1338-1940

Shaw Stewart of Ardgowan papers, 1540-1958

Speirs of Elderslie papers, 1561-1999

GLASGOW UNIVERSITY ARCHIVES
Hillhead Street, Glasgow. G12 8QE
Contains:

Boyd of Trochrig papers, 1485-1759

GLASGOW UNIVERSITY: Record Centre
13 Thurso Street, Glasgow. G11 6PE
Contains:

Beith and other Ayrshire parish papers, 1610-1924

LANARK LIBRARY,
Lindsay Institute, Hope Street, Lanark. ML11 7LZ
Contains:

Record of the Royal Burgh of Lanark, 1150-1975

NORTH LANARKSHIRE ARCHIVES
10 Kelvin Road, Lenziemill, Cumbernauld. G67 2BD
Contains:

Drumpellier estate papers, 1560-1961

Dalzell estate papers, 1413-1940

MOTHERWELL HERITAGE CENTRE
High Road, Motherwell. ML1
Contains:

The Hamilton of Dalzell papers, dating from 1415.

RENFREWSHIRE ARCHIVES
Local Studies Department, Central Library,
6-8 High Street, Paisley. PA1 2BB
Contains:

Renfrew burgh records from 1655

Paisley burgh records from 1594

THE STEWARTRY MUSEUM,
St Mary Street, Kirkcudbright. DG6 4JG
Contains:

Kirkcudbright Town Council records, 1576-1975

STRANRAER MUSEUM,
55 George Street, Stranraer. DG9 7JP
Contains the burgh archives of Stranraer, Wigtown, Newton Stewart
and Whithorn, from the sixteenth century, and protocol books of the
seventeenth century.

Other Sources

Primary source material

Among the documents in the National Archives of Scotland is a
substantial collection entitled ***Papers relating to the Plantation of
Ulster, 1611-1669***, which bears the reference NAS.RH15/91/32-40.
This is a miscellany which includes a list of Scottish freeholders,
inventories, rent rolls, letters, accounts, and also larger documents
such as in the following examples:

*"A Book of Survaie of the lands belonging to the Right Wor-
shipful Companie of Haberdashers, anno 1615, the Ulster Settlement"* [NAS.RH15.91.34].

"A Book of H.M. Grace's sent over by the agents for Ireland, Anno 1629" [NAS.RH15.91.36].

"An Account of moneys paid by Tristram Beresford on account of the Company of Haberdashers in London, 1616" [NAS. RH15.91.35].

Another such collection that can be consulted in the NAS is a massive collection of original manuscripts dating between 1532 and 1814 and pertaining to the counties of Ayr, Wigtown, and Kirkcudbright, call number NAS.RH15.216.

Maps

Researchers wishing to locate sites in Scotland associated with their ancestors generally use the highly detailed Ordnance Survey maps that are commonly and inexpensively available [see www.ordsvy.gov.uk]. The Ordnance Survey department began surveying Scotland in the aftermath of the '45 and within a few years had mapped most of Scotland. Many, if not all, of the Ordnance Survey maps produced in the Victorian period have been republished by David and Charles, Newton Abbot, Devon, England, also try www.old-maps.co.uk, which has a gazetteer and digitised printable historical maps of the nineteenth century. These nineteenth-century maps are invaluable when attempting to find farms, villages, and houses which are no longer in existence as a result of having been demolished or been built over due to industrial expansion or housing estates. However, what is the position for the seventeenth century? Here too, fortunately, relatively highly detailed maps exist for most of Scotland. Scotland by the mid-seventeenth century had become one of the best mapped countries of Europe. The existence of these maps is due to the work of Timothy Pont, who in the late sixteenth century compiled maps of most of Scotland. At the time of his death in 1610, only one of his maps had been published, but his originals were bought by Sir James Balfour who intended to publish them. However, the task of publishing was entrusted to Johann Bleau in Amsterdam. In 1654 Blaeu's *Atlas Novus* volume five was published in Amsterdam entitled *Vyfde Stuck der Aerdrycks Beschryving, welck vervat Schotlandt en Yrlandt.* It contained forty-nine maps of Scotland showing Scotland around the beginning of the seventeenth century and identifying around 20,000 places by name. All areas of south-western Scotland are shown in detail. For those unable to access the originals, now in the National Library of Scotland, probably the best option to consult is Jeffrey Stone's *Illustrated Maps of Scotland from Blaeu's Atlas Novus of the 17th Century* [Studio Editions, London, 1991]. The National Library of Scotland has one of the largest map collections in the world, most of which are located at its Map Library in Edinburgh. Much of its Scottish collection has been digitised and can be viewed on www.nls.uk/digitallibrary/maps, and prints are generally available.

The National Archives of Scotland has a substantial collection of plans, which have been divided into two main series. Register House plans come from a variety of sources dating from around 1750 to 1850, while Sheriff Court plans relate mainly to the development of the railways and other public utilities during the nineteenth century. The first of these may well have material of interest to the family historian as they show houses, farms, road, property boundaries, and various topographical features. However, only a handful of these plans fall within our period 1600 to 1750. Among those belonging to the south western counties are two for Lochmaben, Dumfries-shire:

The first plan is dated 1734 and shows part of the South Common of Lochmaben; it is a commonty plan colored to show the scheme of division. Farms shown include Barlouth, Thorniethwaite, Broadchapped, Hunterhall and Nichols-year. The plan also shows the easterly part of Torthorwald parish [NAS.RHP.218].

The second is dated 1742 and shows the Commonty of Heckbog, and the farms of Greenhill, Priestdykes and Parkend, with the names of adjacent owners [NAS.RHP.200].

Some of the topographical plans contain vignettes showing particular places marked on the document such as farmhouses. Lists of these plans have been published in a series of four books issued by the Scottish Record Office [now the NAS] between 1966 and 1988 entitled *Descriptive List of Plans in the Scottish Record Office.* The plans are listed alphabetically by county and then by parish; each book is comprehensively indexed.

Probably the best source of information on available maps is the two volumes of *The Early Maps of Scotland* published by the Royal Scottish Geographical Society in Edinburgh. Volume One, published in 1973, contains a history of Scottish maps and provides details of over 450 maps issued prior to 1850. Volume Two, dated 1983, contains information on over 2000 items under headings such as marine charts, historical maps, county and town maps, roads and canals, agriculture, and a few estate plans.

For those wishing to know what the towns of seventeenth century Scotland looked like, without doubt the best sources are the contemporary topographical prints by John Slezer which were first published in his *Theatrum Scotiae* [London, 1693].

Prospectus Civitatis AER.E ab Orientale . The Prospect of the Town of AIR from the East.

GLOSSARY AND ABBREVIATIONS

AANHS: Ayr Archaeological and Natural History Society

Bailliary: the district under the jurisdiction of a baillie

Baillie: a burgh magistrate, or an officer of a barony

Barony: the lands held by or the tenure appropriate to a baron

Brother/sister german: born of the same parents

Commonty: land held in common by local land-owners on which vassals or tenants could pasture livestock, dig peat, and collect firewood

Conventicle: a clandestine religious meeting of dissenters

DGNHAS: Dumfries and Galloway Natural History and Archaeological Society

Flesher: a butcher

GAS: Glasgow Archaeological Society

Ilk: of the place of that name, used to distinguish the head of a landed family

Kirk: church

Kirk Session: a committee formed by the parish minister and elders

Lege: legally

Merk: a Scottish coin

Mortcloth: a pall covering a coffin bound for the grave

NAS: the National Archives of Scotland, Edinburgh

Presbytery: a church court responsible for a number of parishes

pp: privately published

Provost: equivalent to a mayor in England

Regality: a district under the jurisdiction of a powerful lord

Reiver: a rustler or bandit

RPCS: Register of the Privy Council of Scotland

Sasine: the act of handing over ownership of feudal property

Sept: a subsidiary and subordinate clan

SGS: Scottish Genealogy Society

SHS: Scottish History Society

SRS: Scottish Record Society

Stewartry: a district under the jurisdiction of a Crown official

Synod: a church court responsible for a number of Presbyteries

Tocher: a bride's dowry

Umquhill: late or deceased

Writer: lawyer

FAMILY HISTORY SOCIETIES
IN SOUTH-WEST SCOTLAND

Alloway and South Ayrshire FHS, Alloway Library, Doonholm Road, Ayr. KA7 4QQ

Dumfries and Galloway FHS, 9 Glasgow Road, Dumfries. DG2 9AF

East Ayrshire FHS, The Dick Institute, Elmbank Avenue, Kilmarnock. KA1 3BU

Glasgow and West of Scotland FHS, Unit 13, 32 Mansdield Street, Glasgow. G11 5QP

Lanarkshire FHS, 26A Motherwell Business Centre, Coursington Road, Motherwell. ML1 1PW

Largs and North Ayrshire FHS, Largs Library, 18 Allanpark Street, Largs. KA30 9AG,

Renfrewshire FHS, P.O.Box 9239, Kilmacolm. PA13 4WZ

Troon and Ayrshire FHS, Troon Public Library, Troon. KA10 6EF

MAIN ARCHIVES AND LIBRARIES
IN SOUTH-WEST SCOTLAND

AYRSHIRE
Ayrshire Archives, Craigie Estate, Ayr. KA8 0SS
East Ayrshire Library, Dick Institute, Kilmarnock. KA1 3BU
East Ayrshire Library, Baird Institute, Cumnock. KA18 1AD
North Ayrshire Library, Carnegie Library, Ayr. KA8 8ED

DUMFRIES-SHIRE, KIRKCUDBRIGHTSHIRE, and
WIGTOWNSHIRE
Dumfries and Galloway Archives, 33 Burns Street, Dumfries. DG1 2PS
Dumfries and Galloway Library, Ewart Library, Catharine Street,
    Dumfries. DG1 1JB

LANARKSHIRE
Glasgow Archives, North Street, Glasgow. G3 7DN
Mitchell Library, North Street, Glasgow. G3 7DN
Caledonian University Library, Cowcaddens Road, Glasgow. G4 0BA
Glasgow University Archives, Hillhead Street, Glasgow. G12 8QE
Strathclyde University Archives, 16 Richmond Street, Glasgow. G1
    1XQ
North Lanarkshire Library, Wellwynd, Airdrie. ML6 0AG
North Lanarkshire Library, High Road, Motherwell. ML1 3HU
South Lanarkshire Library, Lindsay Institute, 16 Hope Street, Lanark.
    ML11 7LZ
South Lanarkshire, Library, Cadzow Street, Hamilton. ML3 6HQ

RENFREWSHIRE
East Renfrew Library, Station Road, Giffnock. G46 6JF
Renfrewshire Archives, High Street, Paisley. PA1 2BB
Watt Library, 9 Union Street, Greenock. PA16 8JH
Paisley University Library, High Street, Paisley. PA1 2BE

WIGTOWNSHIRE
Stranraer Museum, Old Town Hall, Stranraer. DG9 7JP

BIBLIOGRAPHY OF FAMILY HISTORIES
OF SOUTH WESTERN SCOTLAND
PUBLISHED IN GREAT BRITAIN

The following list is of published family histories pertaining to south west Scotland. It is unlikely that any one library in Scotland has a complete collection of these books, except possibly the National Library of Scotland in Edinburgh. The NLS, being a copyright library, in theory should receive a copy of every book published within the United Kingdom. The Mitchell Library in Glasgow claims to be the biggest reference library in Europe and together with the Glasgow Archives, which is adjacent, should provide much primary and secondary source material. Some limited edition books were privately published, often by the author, and can be identified by the abbreviation "pp."

AGNEW
The Agnews of Lochnaw, a history of the hereditary sheriffs of Galloway. Sir Andrew Agnew [pp, Edinburgh, 1864].
A genealogy of the Agnews of Lochnaw, Sir Crispin Agnew [pp, 1977].
Agnew of Kilumquha, R.C Reid, in *Transactions of the Dumfriesshire and Galloway Natural History Society,* 3rd series, volume xxiii [DGNHAS, Dumfries, 1940-4], pp. 151-154.

ANDERSON
Andersons of Dumfries, J. Anderson [pp, Welshpool, 1961].

ARMSTRONG
The Armstrong borderland, W. A. Armstrong [pp, Galashiels, 1960].
The kinsmen of Kinmont Willie, in *Transactions of the Dumfriesshire and Galloway Natural History and Antiquarian Society,* 3rd series, volume xviii [DGNHAS, Dumfries, 1931-3], pp. 62-70.

AUCHENLECK
Genealogical fragments relating to the families of Auchenleck, J. Maidment [pp, Berwick, 1855].

BAIRD
The Bairds of Gartsherrie, A. McGeorge [pp, Glasgow, 1875].

BELL
The Bell family in Dumfries-shire, J. Steuart, in *Records of the Western Marches,* volume ii [pp, Dumfries, 1932].

BIGGAR
The family of Biggar, Stewartry of Kirkcudbright, 1614-1912, G.W. Shirley [pp, Dumfries, 1912].

BLACK
A note on the family of Black of Over Abington, 1694-1924 with memoranda on Willison of Redshaw, Steel of Annathill, and Blackie of Glasgow. W. G. Black [pp, Glasgow, 1908].

BORLAND
The Borland Clan origin and migration from Scotland, J.C.Borland, in *The Scottish Genealogist,* volume xl, 2 [Scottish Genealogy Society, Edinburgh, 1993], pp. 51-58.

BOYD
Annals of the House and family of Boyd, Earls of Kilmarnock and lairds of Penkill Castle and Tochrogue, AD1153-AD1963. F. Cameron [pp, Edinburgh, 1963]
Selection from the papers of the family of Boyd of Kilmarnock, 1468-1590, James Maidment [Abbotsford Club, Edinburgh, 1837].
Boyds of Kilmarnock [Kilmarnock History Group, Kilmarnock, 1980].
The Boyds of Penkill and Trochrig, Seymour Clark [W. Blackwood, Edinburgh, 1909].

BOYLE
Genealogical Account of the Boyles of Kelburne, R. Boyle [T & A Constable, Edinburgh, 1904].

CANNAN
The Cannan family in Galloway, in *Transactions of the Dumfries-shire and Galloway Natural History and Antiquarian Society,* volume xxxi [DGNHAS, Dumfries, 1952-3], pp. 78-120.

CARLISLE
History of the Paisley branch of the Carlisle or Carlile family, J. W. Carlile [pp, Winchester, 1909].

CARRUTHERS
A collection of records setting forth the history of the Carruthers family, Arthur Stanley Carruthers [pp, Purley, 1925].

Records of the Carruthers family, A. S. Carruthers and R. C. Reid [pp, London, 1934].

The descendants of George Carruthers of Brydegill, in *Transactions of the Dumfries-shire and Galloway Natural History and Antiquarian Society,* 3rd series, volume xxxv [DGNHAS, Dumfries, 1956-7], pp. 122-126.

CATHCART
The Cathcarts of Carleton and Killochan, in *Ayrshire Archaeological and Natural History Society Collections,* 2nd series, volume 4 [AANHS, Ayr, 1955-1957], pp. 133-142.

CHALMERS
Notes on the Chalmers families of South Ayrshire, J.G. Wilson, in *The Scottish Genealogist,* volume xxxviii, 3 [Scottish Genealogy Society, Edinburgh, 1991], pp. 93-100.

CLELAND
The ancient family of Cleland; an account of the Clelands of that Ilk, in the county of Lanark; of the branches of Fascine, Monkland, etc., John Burton Cleland [pp, London, 1905].

CORRIE
Record of the Corrie family, 802-1899 [pp, London, 1899].

COULTHART
A genealogical and heraldic account of the Coultharts and Collyn, chiefs of the name, George Parker Knowles [pp, London, 1855].

CRICHTON
Sanquhar and the Crichtons, D. Crichton [pp. Dumfries, 1907].

CURRIE
Curries of Cowal, W. Currie [pp, Dunoon, 1975].

DE SOULIS
The feudal family of de Soulis, in *Transactions of the Dumfries-shire and Galloway Natural History and Antiquarian Society,* 3rd series, volume xxvi [DGNHAS, Dumfries, 1947], pp. 163-193, T. McMichael.

DE VETERIPONT
De Veteripont, in *Transactions of the Dumfries-shire and Galloway Natural History and Antiquarian Society,* 3rd series, volume xxxiii [DGNHAS, Dumfries, 1954], pp. 91-106, R. C. Reid.

DOUGLAS
Drumlanrig Castle and the Douglases, C. T. Ramage [J. Anderson, Dumfries, 1876].
Douglas and the Douglas family, C. C. Riach [pp, Hamilton, 1927].
A history of the Douglas family of Morton in Nithsdale and Fingland, and their descendants, P. W. L. Adams [Sidney Press, Bedford, 1921].
The Black Douglasses and Threave Castle, J. Robison [Castle Douglas, 1911].

DUNLOP
Dunlop of that Ilk: memorabilia of the families of Dunlop, A. Dunlop [pp, Glasgow, 1898].
Dunlop of Dunlop and of Auchenskaith, Keppoch and Gairbraid, A. Dunlop [Butler & Tanner, Frome, 1939].
Record of the Dunlops of Dunlop, R. Reid [pp, Dunmow, 1900].

EDMONSTONE

Genealogical Account of the family of Edmonstone of Duntreath, Sir A. Edmondstone [pp; Edinburgh, 1875].

ELLIOT

The Elliots: the story of a border clan, Sir Arthur and Lady Dora Elliot [Seeley Service & Company, London, 1974].

The Border Elliots and the family of Minto, G. F. S. Elliot [pp, Edinburgh, 1897].

The Elliots of Larriston, E. Barton, in *Transactions of the Hawick Archaeological Society* [HAS, Hawick, 1944], pp. 10-19.

The Elliots of Minto: historical review of a great border family, M. Scott, in *Transactions of the Hawick Archaeological Society* [HAS, Hawick, 1938], pp. 71-78.

Elliot Traditions, F. Elliot [pp, Edinburgh, 1922].

Metrical History of the honourable families of the name of Scot and Elliot in the shires of Roxburgh and Selkirk, W. Scot [pp, Edinburgh, 1892].

GAIRDNER

A chronicle of the family of Gairdner of Ayrshire, Edinburgh and Glasgow, and their connections from the 17th century, W. H. Bailey [Hammett and Company, Taunton, 1947].

GLENDINNING

House of Glendinning, P. Glendinning [Eskdale and Liddesdale Advertiser, Edinburgh, 1879].

The family of Glendonyng, R. C. Reid, in *Transactions of the Dumfries-shire and Galloway Natural History and Antiquarian Society,* 3rd series, volume xxii [DGNHAS, Dumfries, 1938-1940], pp. 10-17.

GRAHAM

The Border Grahams: their origin and distribution, R. C. Reid, in *Transactions of the Dumfries-shire and Galloway Natural History and Antiquarian Society,* 3rd series, volume xxxvii [DGNHAS, Dumfries, 1959], pp. 85-113.

Or and Sable: a book of the Graemes and Grahams. L. G. Graeme [William Brown, Edinburgh, 1903].

HAMILTON

A history of the House of Hamilton, G. Hamilton [pp, Edinburgh, 1933].

A short account of the Hamiltons of Fala and of Fala House, H. H. Dalrymple [pp; 1907].

HANNAY

The Hannays of Sorbie, S. F. B. Francis [Independent Press; London, 1961].

HERIOT

The Heriots of Ramornie from the 15th to the 18th centuries, R. C. Reid [Dumfries, 1931].

HERRIES

Herries of Hartwood, D. C. Herries, in *Transactions of the Dumfries-shire and Galloway Natural History and Antiquarian Society,* 3rd series, volume xxii [DGNHAS, Dumfries, 1938-1940], pp. 35-50.

Herries of Maidenpaup, D. C. Herries, in *Transactions of the Dumfries-shire and Galloway Natural History and Antiquarian Society,* 3rd series, volume xxi [DGNHAS, Dumfries, 1936-1938], pp. 342-359.

HUNTER

Some family papers of the Hunters of Hunterstoun, M. S. Shaw [Scottish Record Society, Edinburgh 1925].

Hunter of Abbotshill, A. A. Hunter [Elliot Stock, London, 1905].

IRVING

Bonshaw Tower: the Irvings and some of their kinsfolk, F. R. Fitzmaurice [Bonshaw Tower; Dumfries, 1898].

The Irvings of Bonshaw, E. J. B. Irving, in *The Scottish Genealogist,* volume xviii, 4 [Scottish Genealogy Society, Edinburgh, 1971], pp. 64-72.

The Irvings of Bonshaw, chiefs of the noble and ancient Scots border family of Irving, A. M. T. Maxwell-Irving [Bletchley Printers, Bletchley, 1968].

The Irvings of Hoddom, G. Irving, in *Transactions of the Dumfries-shire and Galloway Natural History and Antiquarian Society,* volume xvii [DGNHAS, Dumfries, 1900-1905], pp. 175-201.

JOHNSTONE
History of the Johnstones, 1191-1909, C. L. Johnstone [W and A. K. Johnstone, Edinburgh, 1909].

The Annandale family book of the Johnstones, Sir W. Fraser [pp, Edinburgh, 1894].

KERR
Border story: the name and house of Kerr at Monteviot, Jedburgh, the Marquess of Lothian [Kelso Graphics, Jedburgh, 1980].

KIRKO
The Kirkos of Glenesland, Bogrie, Chapel and Sundaywell, Sir P. J. Hamilton-Grierson, in *Transactions of the Dumfries-shire and Galloway Natural History and Antiquarian Society,* 3rd series, volume iii [DGNHAS, Dumfries, 1914-1915], pp. 222-241.

KIRKPATRICK
The early Kirkpatricks, R. C. Reid, in *Transactions of the Dumfries-shire and Galloway Natural History and Antiquarian Society,* 3rd series, volume xxx [DGNHAS, Dumfries, 1951-1952], pp. 61-109.

The Kirkpatricks at Capenoch, 1727-1846, J. Gladstone, in *Transactions of the Dumfries-shire and Galloway Natural History and Antiquarian Society,* 3rd series, volume xv [DGNHAS, Dumfries, 1928-1929], pp. 85-94.

The Killilung Kirkpatricks, H. Kirkpatrick, in *The Scottish Genealogist,* volume xxvi, 4 [Scottish Genealogy Society, Edinburgh, 1979], pp. 103-108.

LAMONT
The Lamont Clan, H. McKechnie [Clan Lamont Society; Edinburgh, 1938].

LAURIE
Lauries of Maxwelton and other Laurie families, I. O. J. Gladstone [Research Publishing, London, 1972].

LITTLE
A Thousand Years – the Littles and their forebears, J.C.Little, in *The Scottish Genealogist*, volume xxxv.2 [Scottish Genealogy Society, Edinburgh, 1988], pp. 45-62.

LOCKHART
Seven centuries: a history of the Lockharts of Lee and Carnwath, S. M. Lockhart [pp, Carnwath, 1976].

LOGAN
Logan of Knockshinnoch [pp, Edinburgh, 1885].

LOVELL
The barony of Hawick and the Lovell family, S. C. Wilson, in *Transactions of the Hawick Archaeological Society* [HAS, Hawick, 1932], pp. 34-39.

LYLE
The Lyles of Renfrewshire, W. Lyle [Glasgow, 1936].

MCCARTNEY
The McCartney Documents, A. E. Truckell, in *Transactions of the Dumfries-shire and Galloway Natural History and Antiquarian Society,* 3rd series, volume lxiv [DGNHS, Dumfries, 1989], pp. 88-90.

MCLELLAN
The McClellans of Gelston, 1264-1610, D. R. Torrance, in *The Scottish Genealogist,* volume xxxiv, 1 [Scottish Genealogy Society, Edinburgh, 1987], pp. 277-285.

The McClellans in Galloway, 2 volumes, D. R. Richard Torrance [Scottish Genealogy Society, Edinburgh, 1993, 1996].

MCTURK
The McTurks of the Glenkens, C.W.Ellis, in *The Scottish Genealogist,* volume xl, 1 [Scottish Genealogy Society, Edinburgh, 1993], pp. 21-27.

MAXWELL
Some Maxwell family histories, D. C. Herries, in *Transactions of the Dumfries-shire and Galloway Natural History and Antiquarian Society,* 3rd series, volume xvi [DGNHAS, Dumfries, 1929-1930], pp. 13-24.

John Maxwell of Castlemilk, R. C. Reid, in *Transactions of the Dumfries-shire and Galloway Natural History Society,* 3rd series, volume xxi [DGNHAS, Dumfries, 1936], pp. 48-58.

The Maxwells of Hazelfield, E. W. J. McConnell, in *Transactions of the Dumfries-shire and Galloway Natural History and Antiquarian Society,* 3rd series, volume xxi [DGNHAS, Dumfries, 1936], pp. 48-58.

The Book of Caerlaverock: memoirs of the Maxwells, Earls of Nithsdale, Lords Maxwell and Herries, Sir W. Fraser [pp, Edinburgh, 1873].

Memoirs of the Maxwells of Pollok, Sir W. Fraser [pp, Edinburgh, 1863].

MOFFAT
Moffat of Cairnbeck, W. A. J. Prevost, in *Transactions of the Dumfries-shire and Galloway Natural History and Antiquarian Society,* 3rd series, volume xxxiii [DGNHAS, Dumfries, 1954], pp. 29-47.

Garwald and the Moffats, W. A. J. Prevost, in *Transactions of the Dumfries-shire and Galloway Natural History and Antiquarian Society,* 3rd series, volume xxix [DGNHAS, Dumfries, 1950-1951], pp. 143-154.

A short history of the family of Moffat of that Ilk, R. M. Moffat [pp, Jersey, 1908].

MONTGOMERIE
Genealogical Account of the Montgomeries of Bridgend of Doon, W. Anderson [pp, Edinburgh, 1859].
Memorials of the Montgomeries, Earls of Eglinton, Sir W. Fraser [pp; Edinburgh, 1859].

MUNDEVILLE
The Mundevilles in Scotland, in *Transactions of the Dumfries-shire and Galloway Natural History and Antiquarian Society,* 3rd series, volume xxxiv [DGNHAS, Dumfries, 1955], pp. 78-83, R. C. Reid.

NEILSON
An account of Neilson of Barncailzie in the parish of Kirkpatrick Durham, Stewartry of Kirkcudbright, W.W.Neilson [pp, Leeds, 1979].
An account of Neilson of Craigcaffie in the parish of Inch, Wigtownshire, W. W. Neilson [pp, Leeds, 1978].
Neilson inventory, R. C. Reid, in *Transactions of the Dumfries-shire and Galloway Natural History and Antiquarian Society,* 3rd series, volume xxxiv [DGNHAS, Dumfries, 1955-1956], pp. 204-208.

NICHOLSON
Memorials of the family of Nicholson of Blackshaw, Dumfries-shire, F. Nicholson [pp, Kendal, 1928].

NISBET
Nisbet of that Ilk, R. C. Nesbitt [John Murray, London, 1941].
Nisbet of Carfin, J. A. Inglis, in *Miscellanea Genealogica et Heraldica,* 5th series, volume ii [Hamilton and Adams, London, 1916-1917], pp. 44-52.

ORR
The Orrs of Kaim, Lochwinnoch parish, Renfrewshire, W. Kerr-Hogarth, in *The Scottish Genealogist*, volume xvii, no.2 [Scottish Genealogy Society, Edinburgh, 1970], pp. 41-48.

PATERSON
Paterson of Kinhervie, R. C. Reid, in *Transactions of the Dumfries-shire and Galloway Natural History and Antiquarian Society,* 3rd series, volume xxxii [DGNHAS, Dumfries, 1953-1954], pp. 132-137.

PAUL
Some relatives of John Paul Jones, R. C. Reid, in *Transactions of the Dumfries-shire and Galloway Natural History and Antiquarian Society,* 3rd series, volume xxiv [DGNHAS, Dumfries, 1945-1946], pp. 79-82.

PRINGLE
Record of the Pringles or Hoppringles of the Scottish border, A. Pringle [Oliver and Boyd, Edinburgh, 1933].

PROUDFOOT
The Proudfoots of Annandale, W. A. J. Prevost, in *Transactions of the Dumfries-shire and Galloway Natural History and Antiquarian Society,* 3rd series, volume xxx [DGNHAS, Dumfries, 1951-1952], pp. 121-131.

RUTHERFORD
Rutherfords of that Ilk, and their cadets, T. H. Cockburn-Hood [pp, Edinburgh, 1884].

SCOTT
The Scotts, J. M. Dunlop. [Edinburgh, 1957]
Metrical History of the honourable families of the name of Scot and Elliot in the shires of Roxburgh and Selkirk, W. Scot [pp; Edinburgh, 1892].
Scott, 1118-1923, a collection of Scott pedigrees, K. S. M. Scott [Burke, London, 1923].
Scott of Wamphrey and their kinsmen, R. C. Reid, in *Transactions of the Dumfries-shire and Galloway Natural History and Antiquarian Society,* 3rd series, volume xxxiii [DGNHAS, Dumfries, 1954-1955], pp. 18-28.

Scotts of Buccleuch, Sir W. Fraser [pp, Edinburgh, 1878].

The Scotts of Harperrig, J. A. Inglis [pp, London, 1914].

Upper Teviotdale and the Scotts of Buccleuch, J. R. S. Oliver [pp, Hawick, 1887].

The Scotts of Euisdail, T. J. Carlyle [Vair & McNairn, Hawick, 1884].

TURNBULL

Turnbulls of Bedrule, in *Transactions of the Hawick Archaeological Society* [HAS, Hawick, 1955], pp. 53-54.

WALLACE

The Wallaces of Elderslie, J. O. Mitchell, in *Transactions of the Glasgow Archaeological Society,* new series, volume I [GAS, Glasgow, 1890], pp. 102-115.

The book of Wallace, C. Rogers [Grampian Club, Edinburgh, 1889].

WILSON

Wilson of Croglin, R. C. Reid, in *Transactions of the Dumfries-shire and Galloway Natural History and Antiquarian Society,* 3rd series, volume xxviii [DGNHAS, Dumfries, 1949-1950], pp. 135-149.

YOUNGER

An account of the family of Younger in the county of Peebles, A.W. C. Hallen [pp; Edinburgh, 1890] .

BIBLIOGRAPHY OF LOCAL HISTORIES
OF SOUTH WESTERN SCOTLAND
PUBLISHED IN GREAT BRITAIN

Family historians wishing to put their genealogy into context need to understand the social and economic history of the burgh or parish where their ancestors lived. Such information can often be located within published local histories. The quality of such books can, however, vary tremendously from a well- researched and referenced work to a superficial anecdotal effort. The following list, alphabetical by location, identifies many of the published local histories relating to south-west Scotland. Virtually every library will have its own local collection, but few will possess the complete list, except perhaps the Mitchell Library and the National Library of Scotland. Some limited edition books were privately published, often by the author, and can be identified by the abbreviation "pp."

Royal Burgh of Ayr, A. I. Dunlop [Ayr Archaeological and Natural History Society, Edinburgh, 1953].

Ayr Burgh Accounts, 1534-1624, G. S. Pryde [Scottish History Society, Edinburgh, 1937].

Ayrshire, its history and historic families, 2 volumes, William Robertson [Kilmarnock, 1908].

The Shipping Trade of Ayrshire, 1689-1791, Eric J. Graham [Ayrshire Antiquarian and Natural History Society, Ayr, 1991].

Archaeological and Historical Collections of Ayr and Wigton, volume IV [Ayr and Galloway Archaeological Association, Edinburgh, 1884].

Douglasdale, its history and traditions, J. D. Hutchison [pp; London, 1940].

The book of Dumbartonshire, J. Irving [pp; Edinburgh, 1879].

Dumbarton Common Good Accounts, 1614-1660, F. Roberts and I. M. M. MacPhail [Lennox Herald, Dunbarton, 1972].

History of the Burgh of Dumfries, W. McDowall [T. Hunter, Dumfries, 1906, and Scolar Press, Menston, 1972].

Crime and Punishment in 17th and 18th century records of Dumfries, M. M. Stewart, in *Transactions of the Dumfries-shire and Galloway Natural History and Antiquarian Society,* 3rd series, volume lxxii [DGNHAS, Dumfries, 1997], pp.69-78; volume lxxiii [DGNHAS, Dumfries, 1999], pp. 195-208.

Some 17th century Custom and Excise Records for Dumfries and Kirkcudbright, A. E. Truckell, in *Transactions of the Dumfriesshire and Galloway Natural History and Antiquarian Society,* 3rd series, volume lxxv [DGNHAS, Dumfries, 2001], pp. 173-176.

Charter chest of the earldom of Dundonald, 1219-1672, F. J. Grant [Scottish Record Society, Edinburgh, 1910].

Our Galloway Ancestors revisited, D. C. Landsborough [pp; Thornton Heath, 1978].

History of the lands and their owners in Galloway, P. H. McKerlie [A. Gardner, Paisley, 1906].

Muniments of the Royal Burgh of Irvine, Volumes I & II [Ayr and Galloway Archaeological Association, Edinburgh, 1890/1891].

Royal Burgh of Irvine, A. F. McJannet [Civic Press, Glasgow, 1938].

History of Irvine, J. Strawhorn [John Donald, Edinburgh, 1985].

Kilmaurs, Parish and Burgh, D. McNaught [A. Gardner, Paisley, 1912].

The Stewartrie of Kirkcudbright court minutes 1670 and 1684, A. E. Truckell, in *Transactions of the Dumfries-shire and Galloway Natural History and Antiquarian Society,* 3rd series, volume lxxv [DGNHAS, Dumfries, 2001], pp. 181-184.

Lanark: the Burgh and its Councils, 1469-1880, A. D. Robertson [Lanark Town Council, Glasgow, 1974].

The Lochmaben Court and Council Book, 1612-1721, John B. Wilson [Scottish Record Society, Edinburgh, 2001].

Royal Burgh of Lochmaben Court and Council Book, 1612-1721, J. B. Wilson, in *Transactions of the Dumfries-shire and Galloway*

Natural History and Antiquarian Society, 3rd series, volume lxv [DGNHAS, Dumfries, 1990], pp. 84-92.

Life in Lochmaben, 1612-1721, J. B. Wilson, in *Transactions of the Dumfries-shire and Galloway Natural History and Antiquarian Society,* 3rd series, volume lxviii [DGNHAS, Dumfries, 1993], pp. 123-130.

Lochwood Tower, R. C. Reid, in *Transactions of the Dumfries-shire and Galloway Natural History and Antiquarian Society,* 3rd series, volume xiii [DGNHAS, Dumfries, 1925-1926], pp. 187-193.

Mouswald Kirk Session Minutes: 1640-1659, A. E. Truckell, in *Transactions of the Dumfries-shire and Galloway Natural History and Antiquarian Society,* 3rd series, volume lxxvii, [DGNHAS, Dumfries, 2003] pp. 167-180.

Scottish Catholic parents and their children, 1701-1705. F. McDonnell [pp, St Andrews, 1995].

Burgh of Paisley poll tax roll, 1695, F. McDonnell [pp, St Andrews, 1995].

Portpatrick Customs, 1671-1699, A. E. Truckell, in *Transactions of the Dumfries-shire and Galloway Natural History and Antiquarian Society,* 3rd series, volume lxxvi [DGNHAS, Dumfries, 2002], pp. 160-161.

Early Stranraer Record, A. E. Truckell, in *Transactions of the Dumfries-shire and Galloway Natural History and Antiquarian Society,* 3rd series, volume lxvi [DGNHAS, Dumfries, 1991], pp. 91-94.

Folklore and genealogies of Upper Nithsdale, W. Wilson [pp, Dumfries, 1904].

The Parish Lists of Wigtownshire and Minnigaff, 1684. W. Scott [Scottish Record Society, Edinburgh, 1916].

Record of the General Assemblies of the Church of Scotland, 1648-1649, A. Mitchell and J. Christie [Edinburgh, 1896].

William Fullarton's Expenses, 1689-1692, about the war in Ireland, A. E. Truckell, in *Transactions of the Dumfries-shire and Galloway Natural History and Antiquarian Society,* 3rd series, volume lxxvi [DGNHAS, Dumfries, 2002], pp. 162-165.

GENERAL BIBLIOGRAPHY

J. Agnew, Belfast Merchant Families in the Seventeenth Century [Four Courts Press, Dublin, 1996].

G. F. Black, The Surnames of Scotland, Their Origin, Meaning and History [New York Public Library, New York, 1946].

K. B. Cory, Tracing your Scottish Ancestry, 3rd edition [Genealogical Publishing Company, Baltimore, 2004].

D. Dobson, Scots-Irish Links, 1575-1725, 5 parts [Clearfield Company, Baltimore, 1997-2006].

R. Gillespie, Colonial Ulster, the settlement of East Ulster, 1600-1641 [Cork University Press, Cork, 1985].

R. Gillespie, Settlement and Survival on an Ulster estate [Public Record Office of Northern Ireland, Belfast, 1988].

J. Grenham, Tracing Your Irish Ancestors, 3rd edition [Genealogical Publishing Company, Baltimore, 2006].

J. K. Hewison, The Covenanters, 2 volumes [J. Smith, Glasgow, 1908].

G. Hill, An historical account of the Plantation in Ulster at the commencement of the seventeenth century, 1608-1620 [Irish University Press, Shannon, 1970 reprint].

C. Humphrey-Smith, The Phillimore Atlas and Index of Parish Registers, 2nd edition [Phillimore, Chichester, 1996].

L. Jonas and P. Milner, A Genealogists's Guide to Discovering Your Scottish Ancestors: How to find and record your unique heritage [F & W Publications, Cincinatti, 2002].

S. Lewis, A Topographical Dictionary of Scotland, 2 volumes [Genealogical Publishing Company, Baltimore, 1989, reprint].

P. McNeill and H. MacQueen, Atlas of Scottish History to 1707 [University of Edinburgh, Edinburgh, 1996].

Sir J. B. Paul, The Scots Peerage [Edinburgh, 1904-1914].

M. Perceval-Maxwell, The Scottish Migration to Ulster in the Reign of James I [Humanities Press, New York, 1973].

M. Robinson, The Concise Scots Dictionary [Aberdeen University Press, Aberdeen, 1985].

A. Rosie, Scottish Handwriting, 1500-1700: a self-help pack [National Archives of Scotland, Edinburgh, 1994].

G. G. Simpson, Scottish Handwriting, 1150-1650, an introduction to the reading of documents [Aberdeen University Press, Aberdeen, 1973].

T. C. Smout, A History of the Scottish People, 1560-1830 [Collins, London, 1969].

D. Stevenson, Scottish Covenanters and Irish Confederates. Scottish-Irish Relations in the mid-seventeenth Century [Ulster Historical Foundation; Belfast, 1981].

F. Wilkins, Scottish Customs and Excise Record, with particular reference to Strathclyde from 1707 onwards [Wyre Forest Press; Kidderminster, 1992].

Descriptive List of Plans in the Scottish Record Office, 4 volumes [National Archives of Scotland, Edinburgh, 1966-1988].

INDEX